Bible Things Quiz Book

Erma Reynolds

BAKER BOOK HOUSE
Grand Rapids, Michigan 49506

Copyright 1981 by
Baker Book House Company

ISBN: 0–8010–7711–7

Printed in the United States of America

1. Ark of the Covenant

1. What talented craftsman was appointed to construct the ark?
2. What wood was used in its construction?
3. What three memorials did the ark contain?
4. What leader used the ark to demonstrate a miracle at the river Jordan?
5. Who captured the ark and kept it for seven months?
6. Who was struck dead because he touched the ark while trying to steady it?
7. Who sheltered the ark in his home for three months?
8. Who returned the ark to Jerusalem?
9. What type of housing was prepared for the ark in Jerusalem?
10. Who were the only persons permitted to carry the ark to its new home?

2. Assemble the Ensemble

Each of the following quotes mention clothing. From the three choices given, see if you can supply the missing word.

1. "Beware of the scribes which love to go in _____ clothing. . . ."
   (a) long   (b) somber   (c) shapeless

2. "They clothed him with _____, and platted a crown of thorns, and put it about his head."
   (a) red   (b) purple   (c) white

3. "And she had a garment of _____ colours upon her. . . ."
   (a) tessellated   (b) divers   (c) variegated

4. "But all their works they do for to be seen of men: they make broad their phylacteries, and enlarge the _____ of their garments."
   (a) train   (b) borders   (c) breastplate

5. "The father said to his servants, Bring forth the _____ robe, and put it on him. . . ."
   (a) best   (b) colored   (c) festive

6. "And ye have respect to him that weareth the _____ clothing. . . ."
   (a) gay   (b) goodly   (c) gorgeous

7. "The king's daughter is all glorious within: her clothing is of wrought _____."
   (a) embroidery   (b) silver   (c) gold

8. "But what went ye out for to see? A man clothed in _____ raiment?"
   (a) strange   (b) dark   (c) soft

9. "Thus saith the LORD unto me, Go and get thee a _____ girdle, and put it upon thy loins, and put it not in water."
   (a) lyssus   (b) leather   (c) linen

10. "She maketh herself coverings of _____. . . ."
    (a) broidered cloth   (b) tapestry   (c) silk

3. Axes

1. During the construction of what building was there no sound of an ax being used?
2. Who took an ax and cut a bough from a tree as an example for his soldiers to follow?
3. After Joab defeated the city of Rabbah, who cut its citizens with axes and saws?
4. In a sermon, who described an ax being laid to tree roots?
5. What psalmist said, "A man was famous according as he had lifted up axes upon the thick trees"?
6. Who performed a miracle by causing an iron ax head, that had fallen into a stream, to float?
7. According to an Israelite law, where was a man to go if his ax head flew off its handle and killed his neighbor?
8. Who, when besieging a city, were forbidden to cut down trees with an ax?
9. Who mentioned the breaking down of Tyre's towers with axes?
10. Where did the Israelites have to go to sharpen their axes?

4. Baked Goods

1. How many women did God say were to "bake your bread in one oven"?
2. Who had a dream of a basket filled with "all manner of bakemeats"?
3. Who baked unleavened bread for two angels?
4. Who baked cakes for her brother?
5. Who woke from a nap and found an angel had left him "a cake baken on the coals"?
6. What ingredient was gathered, ground in mills, or beat in a mortar, and baked in pans?
7. Who was given each day, "a piece of bread out of the bakers' street"?
8. Who had his wife make cakes of fine meal on a hearth to serve to three visitors?
9. Whose duty, in the Lord's house, was to be in charge of "that which is baked in the pan"?
10. Who told the Israelites if a king were appointed he would "take your daughters . . . to be cooks, and to be bakers"?

5. Barley

Each person at the left had a connection with barley, as described at the right. See if you can match them.

1. John
2. Moses
3. Hosea
4. Gideon
5. Absalom
6. Elisha
7. Boaz
8. Ezekiel
9. Solomon
10. Saul

a. He overheard a man describing a dream about barley bread.
b. On God's order, he ate bread made partly of barley for 390 days.
c. His sons were hanged at the beginning of a barley season.
d. He fed barley to 40,000 horses.
e. He winnowed barley at night.
f. He heard a voice in the midst of a beast say, "three measures of barley for a penny."
g. He fed one hundred men with twenty loaves of barley bread and ears of corn.
h. He had his servants burn a man's barley field.
i. Stretching his hand heavenward, he caused a hailstorm that destroyed a barley crop.
j. He bought his wife using barley as part of the purchase price.

6. Baskets

1. Who put the flesh of a kid in a basket and offered it to an angel under an oak?
2. Who was let down a wall in a basket?
3. What prophet told God he saw a basket of summer fruit?
4. Who dreamed he had three white baskets on his head?
5. Who placed a blessing and a curse on a basket?
6. At whose dedication service was bread brought to the tabernacle in a basket?
7. Who was presented with baskets filled with the heads of seventy murdered men?
8. What prophet was shown two baskets of figs by God?
9. After 4,000 people were miraculously fed, how many baskets were filled with pieces of broken meat?
10. After Jesus fed the 5,000 with five loaves and two fishes, how many baskets were filled with leftovers?

7. Beds

Match the people at the left to the correct reference to a bed, listed at the right.

1. Og
2. Jesus
3. Elisha
4. Ishbosheth
5. Isaiah
6. Ahaziah
7. Ahasuerus
8. Pharaoh
9. David
10. Saul

a. He was murdered as he lay on his bed at noontime.
b. He was told there would be frogs in his bed.
c. Weak from hunger, he sat on a witch's bed.
d. His wife put a lifelike dummy in his bed, so he was able to escape an enemy.
e. He had gold and silver beds.
f. He had an iron bed.
g. Injured by a fall, God told him he would never again leave his bed.
h. He described a bed that was "shorter than that a man can stretch himself on it."
i. He told a man to pick up his bed and walk.
j. He was offered use of a guest chamber equipped with bed, table, and stool.

8. Bible Plants

Fill each blank with the name of a Bible plant.

1. Reuben found _____ and brought them to his mother.
2. Job said, "Let _____ grow instead of wheat, and _____ instead of barley."
3. Jonah sat in the shade of a _____.
4. Jesus said that Solomon in all his glory was not arrayed like a _____.
5. Isaiah said the desert would blossom like the _____.
6. _____ was used at Jesus' crucifixion.
7. Solomon mentioned a slothful man's field grown over with _____.
8. Jesus said that the Pharisees tithed _____ and _____.
9. Baby Moses was put in an ark made of _____.
10. The Israelites compared manna to _____.

9. Boats

Here's a quiz about boats and ships during Scripture times. Match the people, listed at the left, to their connection with a vessel, described at the right.

1. Jonah
2. David
3. Noah
4. Jehoshaphat
5. Solomon
6. Jesus
7. Paul
8. Zebedee
9. Isaiah
10. Zebulun

a. He mentioned ambassadors "by the sea, even in vessels of bulrushes upon the waters."
b. He received instructions from God for the design of this boat.
c. His sons left him in a ship with hired servants.
d. He crossed the river Jordan in a ferry boat with his household.
e. He was sleeping in a ship when it was about to break apart during a storm.
f. He was on a ship that broke apart when it hit a sandbar.
g. He had a navy of ships.
h. His father foretold that he "shall be for an haven of ships."
i. He used a boat for a pulpit.
j. His freighters, built to carry gold, were shipwrecked.

10. Book Report

The Scripture people listed at the left had a connection with the books described at the right. See if you can match them.

1. Josiah
2. Ezra
3. Jeremiah
4. Job
5. Jehoiakim
6. Ahasuerus
7. Joshua
8. Moses
9. Paul
10. Ezekiel

a. He tried to get rid of insomnia by having a book read to him.
b. He asked God to blot him out of His book.
c. He wished his enemy had written a book.
d. He was responsible for those "which used curious arts" burning their valuable books.
e. He was given a seven part book that described cities.
f. He ate a scroll and found it was sweet as honey.
g. He stood on a wooden pulpit, in sight of people, and opened a book.
h. He told Seraiah to tie a stone to a book and throw it into a river after he had finished reading it.
i. He cut up a book with a penknife and then burned it.
j. This king, after hearing the words of a book, tore his clothes.

11. Bottles and Cruses

1. What prophet asked for a cruse filled with salt so he could use it to purify poisoned water?
2. Who opened a bottle of milk and gave a thirsty man a drink?
3. Who asked, "Who can stay the bottles of heaven"?
4. What man, sleeping under a tree, awakened to find a cruse of water at his head?
5. What prophet was instructed by God to buy a potter's bottle and then break it?
6. Who advised against putting new wine into old bottles?
7. Who instructed his wife to take a cruse of honey to Ahijah?
8. What servant met David with a supply of food that included a bottle of wine?
9. Who mentioned putting his tears in a bottle?
10. Who gave a woman bread and a bottle of water, and banished her into the wilderness?

12. Bows and Arrows

In Scripture times, bows and arrows were used as weapons of war and as a means to obtain food. At the left are persons who had a tie-in with this equipment, and at the right is the event in which they were involved.

1. Esau
2. Saul
3. Ishmael
4. Elisha
5. Jonathan
6. Jeremiah
7. Ahab
8. Job
9. Josiah
10. David

a. In a song of deliverance, he said, "he sent out arrows, and scattered them."
b. He grew up in the wilderness and became an archer.
c. While disguised, this king was fatally wounded by archers during battle.
d. This man, beset with troubles, said, "the arrows of the Almighty are within me."
e. He was told by his father to use a bow and arrow to obtain venison.
f. This dying prophet told a king to open a window and shoot an arrow from it.
g. He shot three arrows as a signal to his friend to go into hiding.
h. He instructed archers to shoot at Babylon, sparing no arrows.
i. This king was fatally wounded when a chance arrow struck him between his armor joints during battle.
j. This king committed suicide after being badly wounded by Philistine archers.

13. Brass

1. Who made a serpent of brass that could cure snake bites?
2. What persons were forbidden to carry brass money in their purses?
3. What prophet had a vision of brass mountains?
4. Who said, "I am become as sounding brass"?
5. Who wore a helmet and coat of mail made of brass?
6. What blind prisoner was bound with brass fetters?
7. What king replaced Solomon's plundered gold shields with brass shields?
8. Who cast two brass pillars for Solomon?
9. Who asked, "is my flesh of brass"?
10. What king dreamed of a great statue of a man partly made of brass?

14. Bread

At the left are some people who were involved in the bread incidents described at the right. See if you can match them.

1. Elijah
2. Obadiah
3. Joseph
4. Ezekiel
5. Jeremiah
6. Gideon
7. Moses
8. Lot
9. Jacob
10. Elisha

a. He baked unleavened bread for visiting angels.
b. He ate bread on a mountaintop with companions.
c. He was given bread by ravens.
d. He regularly stopped for bread at a woman's home.
e. He was told that God would rain bread from heaven.
f. He was given fresh bread each day while in prison.
g. He was given a recipe for making bread.
h. He fed one hundred prophets bread and water in a cave.
i. He overheard a dream of barley bread.
j. He exchanged bread for cattle.

15. Breakage

The people listed at the left broke various items. Match each to what he broke, listed at the right.

1. Moses
2. Josiah
3. Gideon's men
4. Hezekiah
5. Woman of Bethany
6. Samson
7. Paul
8. Capernaum citizens
9. Israelites
10. Sodomites

a. Door
b. Withs
c. Roof
d. Idolatrous altars
e. Bread
f. Tables of testimony
g. Gold earrings
h. Moses' brasen serpent
i. Pitchers
j. Alabaster box of ointment

16. Cakes

1. Who said, "Ephraim is a cake not turned"?
2. Who were instructed to take fine flour and bake twelve cakes?
3. Who asked a widow to make him a little cake?
4. Who told his wife to quickly take three measures of flour, knead it and make some cakes for visitors?
5. Who did the Lord say was to receive a cake of oiled bread, and use it as part of a wave offering?
6. What woman included two hundred cakes of figs among provisions she gave to pacify an angry man?
7. What was the taste of the cakes of manna baked by the Israelites?
8. What prophet mentioned women kneading dough to make cakes for the queen of heaven?
9. Who gave a piece of fig cake to an Egyptian found in a battlefield?
10. Who overheard a man relating a dream in which a cake of barley bread tumbled into a tent, overturning it?

17. Candles and Candlesticks

1. Who made a candlestick of pure gold for the ark of the covenant?
2. What prophet had a room furnished for him that included a candlestick?
3. How many gold candlesticks did Solomon have made for his temple?
4. Who saw a man's fingers writing on a wall near a candlestick?
5. In Revelation, how many candlesticks stood before the God of earth?
6. Where did Jesus say men should not hide a candle?
7. What city did Zephaniah say God would search with candles?
8. Who said, "When his candle shined upon my head"?
9. In a prayer of praise, who said, "For thou wilt light my candle"?
10. In Jesus' parable what was lost that a woman looked for with a candle?

18. Cedar

1. Who said, "I dwell in an house of cedar"?
2. According to the Israelites' law, what person was to use cedar wood to cleanse a leprous house?
3. Who, in a parable, described cedars being devoured by fire?
4. What place was celebrated for its cedars?
5. What prophet was told by God, "I will plant in the wilderness the cedar"?
6. What king, when challenged by Amaziah to battle, mentioned the cedar in his refusal to fight?
7. Who, in a song, described the fragrance of cedars?
8. What prophet described cedars being used to make ships' masts?
9. What king supplied cedar trees for construction purposes?
10. During a prophecy, which soothsayer mentioned "cedar trees beside the waters"?

19. Chariots

Chariots in Scripture times were used for both war and peaceful purposes. Match the people at the left to their chariot incident listed at the right.

1. Jehu
2. Sisera
3. Ahab
4. Naaman
5. King Hanun
6. Joseph
7. Pharaoh
8. Elijah
9. Solomon
10. Ethiopian eunuch

a. He lost six hundred chariots in a sea.
b. He built cities in which to keep his chariots.
c. He started out in a chariot for a reunion with his father.
d. He hired 32,000 chariots.
e. He owned nine hundred iron chariots.
f. He was wounded and died in his chariot.
g. He jumped from his chariot and ran to meet a servant.
h. He sat in a chariot and read a book.
i. He had the reputation of being a fast chariot driver.
j. He went to heaven in a chariot of fire.

20. Coats

1. What boy received a new coat every year?
2. What did Jesus say to do if a man took away one's coat?
3. What maker of coats and garments was raised from the dead?
4. How was Aaron's coat to be decorated?
5. How many coats were the disciples forbidden to take on their journeys?
6. Whose variegated coat caused a family feud?
7. Who said, "He that hath two coats, let him impart to him that hath none"?
8. Who had a coat minus seams?
9. Who were bound in their coats before being submitted to a terrible punishment?
10. What material was used to make the first coats?

21. The Color Red

Red was a favorite color in biblical times. At the left are ten red items associated with the people listed at the right. See if you can match them.

1. Scarlet outfit with gold chain
2. Scarlet thread
3. House painted vermilion
4. Red heifer
5. Red hair
6. Scarlet robe
7. Red dragon
8. Red eyes
9. Red pottage
10. Red horses

a. Rahab
b. Eleazar
c. Jesus
d. John
e. Esau
f. Judah
g. Jeremiah
h. Jacob
i. Zechariah
j. Daniel

22. Commercial Articles

In Scripture times a variety of merchandise was imported and exported. Hidden in each of the following sentences, in consecutive letters found in one, two, or three words, is one of these commercial articles. See how many you can discover.

1. For grinding and pounding grain in a mortar, a pestle was used.
2. On Aaron's rod, or club, almonds grew.
3. By wearing old clothes, the Gibeonites tried to trick Joshua.
4. Among the captive Jews living in Babylon, each one yearning to return to Jerusalem was permitted to go.
5. The Lord abhors evasiveness in man.
6. Solomon used fir on the ceilings of his temple.
7. Isaiah mentioned a carpenter using a line, notching, and carving a man's figure.
8. Simon told Jesus he had toiled all night and taken no fish.
9. In the summer months, in the tabernacle's shadow heat was not as uncomfortable.
10. Grain grew in every farmer's field in Scripture times.

23. Cooking Equipment

Hidden in the sentences below are names of utensils and cooking equipment used in biblical times. See how many you can discover.

1. Abraham had Ishmael exiled because he mocked Isaac.
2. Jacob selected spotted goats from Laban's flocks.
3. The golden calf made by the Israelites was ground to powder and splattered on water.
4. After the flood, a rainbow, lovely to see, appeared as a token of God's covenant.
5. Jesus had sharp answers for scribes and Pharisees.
6. Isaiah prophesied about pitch eradicating the land.
7. Because of his cupidity, Gehazi was stricken with leprosy.
8. Ahab, a son of Omri, turned out to be a wicked king.
9. Proverbs says, "Love not sleep lest thou come to poverty."
10. Deborah sang, "As I, even I, will sing unto the Lord."

24. Cords and Ropes

1. Who made a scourge of small cords and used them to drive moneychangers from a temple?
2. What prophet said, "thou shalt have none that shall cast a cord by lot in the congregation of the LORD"?
3. Who bound a man with new ropes?
4. Who asked if a leviathan could be caught by putting a cord around his tongue?
5. Who was let down by cords into a dungeon?
6. Who was with soldiers when they cut off the ropes of a boat?
7. Whose palace had hangings fastened with cords of fine linen?
8. Who let spies "down by a cord through the window"?
9. Whose servants put ropes on their heads and came as suppliants to a king of Israel?
10. Who said a three-fold cord is not quickly broken?

25. Crowns

1. Who saw a vision of twenty-four elders clothed in white with golden crowns on their heads?
2. What queen was commanded to put on her crown and parade her beauty before guests?
3. Who said the Lord was going to give him a crown of righteousness?
4. What little prince, about to become king, had to be surrounded by guards before it was safe to place the crown upon his head?
5. What prophet was told to take gifts of gold and silver, and make them into a crown for Joshua's head?
6. What high priest wore a crown bearing the words, "Holiness to the Lord"?
7. What king was crowned by his mother on his wedding day?
8. What prophet quoted God as saying to the wicked prince of Israel, "Remove the diadem, and take off the crown"?
9. What dead king's crown and bracelets were removed as proof that he was dead?
10. What king had the bejeweled gold crown of a conquered king placed upon his head?

26. Cups

The Bible contains numerous references to cups. See if you can unscramble the words in the following sentences.

1. "Babylon hath been a ENGLOD cup in the LORD'S hand. . . ."
2. "I will take the cup of SITOLAVAN, and call upon the name of the LORD."
3. ". . . Neither shall men give them the cup of CNTIOLNSOAO to drink for their father or for their mother."
4. "The cup of LGNESISB which we bless, is it not the communion of the blood of Christ?"
5. "Thou shalt be filled with drunkenness and sorrow, with the cup of TTSOSINNHAME and desolation. . . ."
6. ". . . Stand up, O Jerusalem, which hast drunk at the hand of the LORD the cup of his RYFU. . . ."
7. "Ye cannot drink the cup of the Lord, and the cup of ILVSED. . . ."
8. "Behold, I will make Jerusalem a cup of ERMTLINGB unto all the people round about. . . ."
9. "For whosoever shall give you a cup of RAWTE to drink in my name, because ye belong to Christ, verily I say unto you, he shall not lose his reward."
10. "The same shall drink of the wine of the wrath of God, which is poured out without mixture into the cup of his DNATIOIGNNI. . . ."

27. Ephods

1. Who wore the first ephod?
2. What color was it?
3. What was engraved on the stone that decorated the shoulders?
4. What craftsman made the ephod?
5. Who had an ephod made from gold earrings taken from enemy Midianites?
6. Who had his ephod, teraphim, and graven image taken from him by five enemy spies?
7. What child wore a linen ephod?
8. What priest brought an ephod to David to be used as an oracle?
9. Who killed eighty-five priests who wore linen ephods?
10. Who, wearing a linen ephod, "danced before the LORD with all his might"?

28. Figs

1. Who prescribed "a lump of figs" as a cure for boils?
2. Who made aprons from fig leaves?
3. Who came to a fig tree that had nothing on it but leaves?
4. What prophet had a vision of two baskets of figs being set before the temple of the Lord?
5. What woman gave David two hundred cakes of figs?
6. Who related a parable in which trees said to the fig tree, "Come thou, and reign over us"?
7. Who disapproved of people bringing "wine, grapes, and figs" into Jerusalem on the sabbath?
8. Who was found in a field and given "a piece of a cake of figs"?
9. Who did Jesus see under a fig tree?
10. Who brought back grapes, pomegranates, and figs from Canaan?

29. Favored with Gifts

The persons at the left gave the gifts, listed by their name, to the people at the right. See if you can match the gifts to their receivers.

1. Jacob—cattle
2. Jeroboam—eatables
3. Joseph—changes of clothing
4. Caleb—springs of water
5. Asa—gold and silver
6. Queen of Sheba—spices
7. Abraham's servant—jewelry
8. Solomon—cities
9. Wise men—gold, frankincense, myrrh
10. Jonathan—clothing and weapons

a. Rebekah
b. Hiram
c. Solomon
d. Ahijah
e. David
f. Jesus
g. Esau
h. Benjamin
i. Ben-hadad
j. Achsah

30. Fiery Furnaces

1. Who, when the sun went down, had a vision of a smoking furnace?
2. What king used a furnace for punishment purposes?
3. What prophet mentioned using a furnace for smelting silver?
4. What mountain had smoke billowing up from it as from a furnace?
5. Who said, "Thou shalt make them as a fiery oven"?
6. Smoke, as from a furnace, rose from what burning cities?
7. What three men were cast into a fiery furnace?
8. In which of Jesus' parables did he mention offending things being cast into a furnace of fire?
9. Who was told to take furnace ashes and toss them into the sky while a king watched?
10. Who, at the dedication of a wall, started out from the "tower of the furnaces"?

31. Fruit

1. What king tried to buy a man's vineyard so he could turn it into an herb garden?
2. Who gave a starving Egyptian servant fruit to eat?
3. What prophet mentioned locusts ruining an apple crop?
4. What hungry man looking for food found a fig tree with nothing on it but leaves?
5. Who planted the first vineyard?
6. Who first made the mistake of eating forbidden fruit?
7. What kind of fruit was the decorative motif on a high priest's robe?
8. Who interpreted a dream about grapes?
9. What travelers longed for melons to eat?
10. What woman gave a gift of food that included one hundred clusters of raisins?

32. Get the Point?

This quiz concerns some Scripture folk and their use of a pointed instrument. These devices are listed at the left, while the people who used them are listed at the right. See if you can match them.

1. Javelin
2. Ox goad
3. Penknife
4. Nail
5. Darts
6. Spear
7. Knife
8. Arrows
9. Dagger
10. Sword

a. Peter
b. Abraham
c. Saul
d. Ehud
e. Shamgar
f. Jael
g. Jehoiakim
h. Benaiah
i. Joab
j. Jehu

33. The Golden Corn

See if you can match the people in the left-hand column to the corn quotation that concerns them.

1. Jesse
2. Boaz
3. Jacob
4. Jesus
5. Woman
6. Pharaoh
7. Samson
8. Joseph
9. Israelites
10. Man from Baalshalisha

a. ". . . went on the sabbath day through the corn. . . ."
b. ". . . gathered corn as the sand of the sea. . . ."
c. ". . . brought the man of God . . . full ears of corn in the husk thereof."
d. "And they did eat of the old corn of the land on the morrow after the passover. . . ."
e. ". . . he let them go into the standing corn of the Philistines, and burnt up both the shocks, and also the standing corn. . . ."
f. ". . . Take now for thy brethren an ephah of this parched corn . . . and run to the camp to thy brethren."
g. "And he slept and dreamed . . . and, behold, seven ears of corn came up upon one stalk. . . ."
h. ". . . took and spread a covering over a well's mouth, and spread ground corn thereon. . . ."
i. ". . . he reached her parched corn. . . ."
j. ". . . I have heard that there is corn in Egypt. . . ."

34. Golden Possessions

Scripture folk treasured their golden possessions. At the left are persons who had some of these precious items, and at the right the variety of golden article, or articles, each possessed. See if you can match them correctly.

1. Nebuchadnezzar
2. Jeroboam
3. David
4. Ahasuerus
5. Shishak
6. Gideon
7. Aaron
8. Job
9. Daniel
10. Solomon

a. Gold crown
b. Gold bed
c. One hundred gold bowls
d. Gold statue
e. Two gold calves
f. Gold earrings
g. Garment trimmed with gold bells
h. Gold chain
i. Gold shields
j. Gold ephod

35. Grains

1. Who was threshing wheat when he saw an angel?
2. Who had his servants set a man's barley field afire?
3. Who threshed wheat by a winepress to hide it from Midianites?
4. During the Egyptian plague of hail, what two grains were destroyed?
5. Which disciple did Jesus say Satan wanted to have so he might sift him as wheat?
6. What stalks of grain did Rahab use to hide two spies?
7. Who set fire to a grain field by tying firebrands between the tails of pairs of foxes?
8. Who winnowed barley at night?
9. Who had phenomenal crops—one hundred times the grain he had sown?
10. Who, during a wheat harvest, prayed to God to send thunder and rain as a means to punish the Israelites?

36. Grains of Salt

1. Who used salt to sweeten brackish spring waters?
2. Who did Jesus describe as the "salt of the earth"?
3. Who regarded food as tasteless unless it was seasoned with salt?
4. What king sowed the captured city of Shechem with salt?
5. What king killed 10,000 Edomites in the Valley of Salt?
6. Who was given the kingdom of Israel with a covenant of salt?
7. What prophet mentioned the custom of rubbing newborn infants with salt?
8. Who was turned into a pillar of salt?
9. Who said every sacrifice would be "salted with salt"?
10. On what food offering were the Israelites instructed by God to put salt?

37. Grass

1. On which day did God create grass?
2. What two men searched for grass to save their horses?
3. Who mentioned a behemoth eating grass?
4. What king ate grass as oxen?
5. Who said, "Let them be as the grass upon the house tops, which withereth afore it groweth up"?
6. Who had a vision of green grass being destroyed by hail and fire?
7. How many people sat on the grass and were miraculously fed?
8. Who mentioned the grass which ". . . is cast into the oven"?
9. Who were promised "grass in thy fields for thy cattle"?
10. What prophet, in a vision, saw grasshoppers eating grass?

38. Honey and the Honeycomb

1. What blind prophet was given honey by a king's wife?
2. Who ate honey from the carcass of a slain lion?
3. Who almost lost his life because he ate honey on the end of a stick?
4. Who was given a honeycomb and a piece of broiled fish to eat?
5. Who did Moses refer to when he sang, "he made him to suck honey out of the rock"?
6. Who ate locusts and wild honey in the wilderness?
7. What land was described as "flowing with milk and honey"?
8. Who said, "it is not good to eat much honey"?
9. Who ate a scroll and found it tasted sweet as honey?
10. What father sent sons to Egypt, carrying a gift of food that included honey?

39. Idol Worship

The idol, or image, was used as an object of worship. At the left are persons who had an involvement with an idol, and at the right are descriptions of these incidents. See if you can match them.

1. Nebuchadnezzar
2. Aaron
3. Laban
4. Hezekiah
5. Asa
6. Micah
7. Jeroboam
8. Ahaz
9. Moses
10. Jacob

a. He instructed his household to get rid of their idols, take a bath, and change their clothes.
b. Five spies entered his house and stole his idols.
c. This wicked king burned his children in fire and made molten images for Baalim.
d. He had a golden calf made from earrings.
e. He had two golden calves made and set up, one in Bethel and the other in Dan.
f. He had a huge golden idol set up in the plain of Dura.
g. He was instructed by God to destroy all the molten images of the Canaanites.
h. He broke in pieces the brazen serpent that Moses had made.
i. He had his images stolen by his daughter.
j. He removed his mother the queen from her throne because she had made an idol in a grove.

40. In the Bag

Bags made of skin, woven material, or formed by folds in a girdle, had various uses in Scripture times. These questions relate to some of these bags.

1. Who placed two talents of silver in two bags and gave them to a servant?
2. Who found a silver cup in his sack?
3. Who put five smooth stones in a shepherd's bag?
4. What prophet mentioned a bag with holes?
5. Who were instructed to provide themselves with "bags which wax not old"?
6. Which prophet referred to a bag containing gold?
7. Who was told, "Thou shalt not have in thy bag divers weights, a great and a small"?
8. Who said his transgression was sealed in a bag?
9. Who carried the disciples' funds in a bag, and often dipped into it for his own use?
10. To deceive Joshua, who visited him wearing old clothes, with old saddlebags on their donkeys?

41. In Great Abundance

Each person at the left had an abundance of an item, or items, listed at the right. See if you can match them.

1. Queen of Sheba   a. Sheep and oxen
2. Israelites   b. Royal wine
3. Solomon   c. Horses
4. Nebuchadnezzar   d. Timber
5. David   e. Riches and honor
6. Ahab   f. Flocks and herds
7. Jehoshaphat   g. Fruit trees
8. Ahasuerus   h. Vessels
9. Huram   i. Iron and brass
10. Hezekiah   j. Spices

42. Jesus' Symbolism

Hidden in each of the following sentences, in consecutive letters found in one, two, or three words, is a symbol pertaining to Jesus. Use the word bank to help you find these hidden words.

Branch	Bread	Door	Lamb	Lion
Rock	Root	Star	Stone	Vine

1. Adam had a rib ready and waiting to make Eve.
2. Jesus said, "blest are the peacemakers."
3. Eli, on hearing the ark was captured, fell and broke his neck.
4. Martha had to do ordinary household chores while her sister sat at Jesus' feet.
5. After getting his father's blessing, Jacob ran, chiefly to escape his brother's wrath.
6. Jesus said first one should remove the beam in his own eye before trying to get a mote out of his brother's eye.
7. The law of Moses forbade a man wearing a woman's frock.
8. Noah was kept busy leading animals to and fro, otherwise the ark would not have been loaded properly.
9. The tribe of Levi needed housing near the tabernacle because they were appointed to care for it.
10. Jezebel used flim-flam by writing letters in Ahab's name and sealing them with his seal.

43. Jewelry Display

See if you can match the people at the left to their particular jewelry incident, listed at the right.

1. Aaron
2. David
3. Rebekah
4. Isaiah
5. Daniel
6. Gideon
7. Ahasuerus
8. Paul
9. Jacob
10. John

a. Made an ephod from gold earrings captured from enemy Ishmaelites.
b. Disapproved of women wearing gold and pearls.
c. Warned that God would take away the jewelry of the daughters of Zion.
d. Hid earrings under a tree.
e. Gave his signet ring to two different men.
f. Had a vision of a city wall inlaid with gems, with each gate a pearl.
g. Given a bracelet and crown as proof a king was dead.
h. Received earrings and bracelets from a thirsty traveler.
i. Rewarded with a gold chain for interpreting handwriting.
j. Melted down earrings to make a golden calf.

44. Kings' Things

Certain items are associated with Biblical kings. Match these kings, listed at the left, to their possession, listed at the right.

1. Ahab
2. Og
3. Ahaz
4. Ahasuerus
5. Sisera
6. Nebuchadnezzar
7. Solomon
8. Jehoiakim
9. Saul
10. David

a. Penknife
b. Javelin
c. Ivory house
d. Gold crown set with gems
e. Ivory throne overlaid with gold
f. 900 iron chariots
g. Golden sceptre
h. Iron bedstead
i. Golden image ninety feet high and nine feet wide
j. Sundial

45. Lamplight

1. What military leader armed his men with lamps inside empty pitchers?
2. Who had a vision of seven lamps of fire burning before a throne?
3. How many virgins, carrying lamps, were mentioned in Jesus' parable?
4. Who had a vision of a burning lamp passing between the halves of carcasses?
5. Who made seven gold lamps for the tabernacle?
6. Who said, "For thou art my lamp, O LORD"?
7. Who had the task of lighting the tabernacle lamps?
8. What prophet told an angel he could see a golden lampstand holding seven lamps being fed with olive oil?
9. Who heard God describe a leviathan as having burning lamps going out of his mouth?
10. What prophet had a vision of strange creatures that glowed like lamps?

46. The Light of the Moon

1. Who had a dream in which the moon bowed to him?
2. Who planned to hide in a field at the time of the new moon?
3. Who ordered the moon to stand still?
4. On what day did God create the moon?
5. Who, at the time of the new moon, offered burnt offerings to God in a temple?
6. What prophet asked, "When will the new moon be gone, that we may sell corn?"
7. Who, in a vision, saw the moon become blood red?
8. How were the Israelites to be punished if they were found worshiping the moon?
9. Who mentioned the moon as "walking in brightness"?
10. What reformer king had all the equipment used in moon worship, destroyed?

47. Little Things

Fill in the blanks in the quotations with words from the word bank.

| Book | Chamber | Coat | Conies | Fishes |
| Flock | House | Lamb | Owl | Ship |

1. "And the little _____, and the cormorant."
2. "'How many loaves have ye?' And they said, 'Seven and a few little _____.'"
3. "His mother made him a little _____."
4. "He had in his hand a little _____."
5. "There be four things which are little upon the earth, but they are exceeding wise: The ants . . . The _____ . . . The locusts . . . The spider."
6. "Fear not, little _____; for it is your Father's good pleasure to give you the kingdom."
7. "Every little _____ was one reed long."
8. "And the other disciples came in a little _____."
9. "The LORD commandeth, and he will smite . . . the little _____ with clefts."
10. "But the poor man had nothing, save one little ewe _____."

48. Lock and Key

1. Which murdered king's body was discovered after his servants took a key and opened a locked room?
2. Who gave orders that Jerusalem's gates were to be closed and locked while guards were still on duty?
3. Who received the keys of the kingdom of heaven?
4. Who conquered the sixteen cities of king Og which were fortified with barred gates and high walls?
5. Who did Jesus say had taken away the key of knowledge?
6. Who said that God had "broken the gates of brass, and cut the bars of iron in sunder"?
7. Who saw "an angel come down from heaven, having the key of the bottomless pit . . . in his hand"?
8. Who was to receive the key to the house of David after he was taken from Shebna?
9. In the repair of Jerusalem's wall, who was responsible for installing locks and bars on the Valley Gate?
10. How many times after his resurrection did Jesus join his disciples, even though they were meeting behind locked doors?

49. Lost and Found

1. Who was sent out to look for his father's lost asses?
2. Who found mandrakes in a field?
3. What did a woman use to look for a lost piece of silver?
4. Who found money in the mouths of sacks?
5. Whose servants accused him of losing his army?
6. Who found the new jawbone of an ass?
7. In Jesus' parable of the lost sheep, how many sheep did the man lose?
8. Who found a wild vine in a field?
9. Who said, "I have gone astray like a lost sheep"?
10. Who found "the book of the law"?

50. Meat on the Menu

1. What prophet boiled meat and bones together to dramatize a parable?
2. Who complained about not having meat to eat?
3. Who killed his oxen and prepared a cookout for plowmen before he started on a journey with a prophet?
4. Who was served fatted calf when he returned home from a long trip?
5. Who ate calf cooked by a witch?
6. Whose favorite meat was venison?
7. What prophet served a king a choice shoulder cut of meat?
8. Who were the only persons permitted to eat the meat of the ram of consecration?
9. Who served cooked calf under a tree to three strangers?

51. The Mighty Oak

1. Who served food to an angel under an oak tree?
2. What nurse was buried under an oak tree?
3. Who buried idols and earrings under an oak?
4. What prophet was told by God, "Yet destroyed I the Amorite . . . he was strong as the oaks"?
5. What people made oars from the oaks of Bashan?
6. What man, as his mule went under the boughs of an oak tree, had his hair caught in its branches?
7. Who found a man of God sitting under an oak and invited him to his home to eat bread?
8. Who rolled a huge stone under an oak tree as a reminder of a covenant's renewal?
9. What slain king and his three sons were buried beneath an oak at Jabesh?
10. On whose farm did an angel sit under an oak tree?

52. Miraculous Foods

1. Who, after being miraculously fed by an angel, was able to travel for forty days and nights on the strength of the one meal?
2. What "small round thing" was miraculously supplied by God to feed the Israelites for forty years?
3. What poisoned food was miraculously made harmless by Elisha?
4. What foodstuffs did Elijah miraculously increase for a widow?
5. What bird was miraculously supplied to feed the hungry Israelites?
6. What birds supplied Elijah with bread and meat twice a day?
7. How many men did Elisha miraculously feed with only twenty small loaves of bread and some ears of corn?
8. Who watched as an angel did miraculous things to roast goat and unleavened bread?
9. How many people did Jesus miraculously feed with only five small loaves of bread and two fishes?
10. When Jesus miraculously fed over 4,000 people with seven loaves of bread and a few fish, how many baskets were filled with leftovers?

53. The Miraculous Manna

1. Why was manna sent by God?
2. What time of day was it first found?
3. What did manna look like?
4. What seed did it resemble?
5. What did it taste like?
6. When were the Israelites to gather it?
7. How much was to be gathered for each person?
8. On which day were they to gather an extra portion?
9. Who was instructed by Moses to put an omer of manna in a pot and keep this in a sacred place as a memorial for future generations?
10. How long did the Israelites eat manna?

54. Nests

Nests, and where they were located during Scripture times is the topic of this quiz. From the word bank, select the correct location for each nest, and fit the word into the proper blank space.

Altars	Boughs	Cedars	Fir trees	Ground
High	Hole's mouth	Rock	Stars	Tree

1. "... and thou puttest thy nest in a _____...."
2. "... thou set thy nest among the _____...."
3. "If a bird's nest chance to be before thee in the way in any _____...."
4. "O inhabitant of Lebanon, that maketh thy nest in the _____...."
5. "All the fowls of heaven make their nests in his _____...."
6. "... like the dove that maketh her nest in the sides of the _____."
7. "... as for the stork, the _____ are her house."
8. "Doth the eagle mount up ... and make her nest on _____?"
9. "If a bird's nest chance to be before thee ... on the _____...."
10. "... the swallow a nest for herself, where she may lay her young, even thine _____, O Lord of Hosts...."

55. New Things

Each person, or persons, at the left did something with a new item. Their actions are listed at the right. See if you can match them.

1. Ahijah
2. Israelites
3. Gibeonites
4. Samson
5. Delilah
6. Sons of Abinadab
7. Princes of Judah
8. Elisha
9. Jesus
10. Twenty-four elders

a. Sat down in the entry of a new gate of the Lord's house.
b. Gave a new commandment.
c. Drove a new cart.
d. Bound a man with new ropes.
e. Offered a new meat offering unto the Lord.
f. Filled new bottles with wine.
g. Killed 1,000 men with the new jawbone of an ass.
h. Sang a new song.
i. Tore a new garment into twelve pieces.
j. Called for a new cruse with salt in it.

56. Noah's Ark

It's a well-known fact that Noah built an ark, but not everyone is knowledgeable about other facts concerning his boat and the flood. Choose the correct answer for each question.

1. How many cubits long was Noah's ark?
    (a) 350   (b) 400   (c) 300
2. What kind of wood went into its construction?
    (a) cedar   (b) gopher   (c) oak
3. How many doors did it have?
    (a) four   (b) one   (c) two
4. How old was Noah when he boarded the ark?
    (a) 300 years   (b) 600 years   (c) 700 years
5. Who closed thé door of the ark?
    (a) God   (b) Noah   (c) Shem
6. How long after the passengers went aboard the ark did it begin to rain?
    (a) five days   (b) six days   (c) seven days
7. How long did the flood waters cover the earth?
    (a) 150 days   (b) 140 days   (c) 130 days
8. On what mountain did the ark come to rest?
    (a) Sinai   (b) Tabor   (c) Ararat
9. What bird did Noah send out first?
    (a) dove   (b) raven   (c) gull
10. What was Noah's first act upon leaving the ark?
    (a) built an altar   (b) said a prayer of thanks
    (c) checked their location

57. Oil

1. What two prophets performed miracles involving oil?
2. What king received twenty measures of pure oil each year as payment for supplying laborers and lumber to a king?
3. How many virgins forgot to take oil for their lamps?
4. Who poured healing oil on a man's wounds?
5. What king laid up stores of oil in fortified cities?
6. What woman did Joab tell to anoint herself with oil, put on mourning clothes, and pretend to be a mourner?
7. What food of the traveling Israelites tasted like fresh oil?
8. Who poured oil over a stone he had used for a pillow?
9. Who was given instructions from God for making holy anointing oil?
10. Who said, ". . . and the rock poured me out rivers of oil"?

58. Olive Trees

Each person, listed at the left, had something to do with an olive tree. Match each to the sentence, listed at the right, that correctly applies.

1. Moses
2. Samson
3. Jeremiah
4. Jesus
5. Solomon
6. David
7. Zechariah
8. Paul
9. Jotham
10. Noah

a. While preaching he mentioned grafting an olive tree.
b. He spent nights on the mount of Olives.
c. He destroyed olive trees by letting burning foxes run through them.
d. He told the Israelites they would acquire olive trees that they had not planted.
e. He said, "The LORD called thy name, A green olive tree, fair, and of goodly fruit."
f. He related a fable about an olive tree.
g. He compared himself to a green olive tree.
h. He used olive wood in constructing a temple.
i. He welcomed a dove carrying an olive leaf.
j. He had a vision of two olive trees on a lampstand.

59. One and Only

It has been said that there are 2,300 words that are mentioned only once in the Bible. Underscored in the questions below are some of these words. See if you can identify the person involved with each word.

1. What prophet announced that God would search Jerusalem with <u>candles</u>?
    (a) Habakkuk   (b) Malachi   (c) Zephaniah
2. What scribe stood upon a wooden <u>pulpit</u> set up in the street?
    (a) Silas   (b) Ezra   (c) Stephen
3. Who made a <u>scaffold</u>?
    (a) Solomon   (b) Haman   (c) Saul
4. Who dreamed of a <u>ladder</u>?
    (a) Nebuchadnezzar   (b) Jacob   (c) Joseph
5. Who used the word <u>chickens</u> in a sermon?
    (a) Jesus   (b) Moses   (c) Job
6. What prophet, while rebuking the sins of Israel, mentioned <u>fishhooks</u>?
    (a) Hosea   (b) Micah   (c) Amos
7. What king used a <u>penknife</u> to cut up a book?
    (a) Jehoiakim   (b) Jeroboam   (c) Jehoahaz
8. What person, angry with Job, described the sky as a molten <u>looking glass</u>?
    (a) Bildad   (b) Zophar   (c) Elihu
9. Who cured sick people by touching them with his <u>handkerchief</u>?
    (a) Paul   (b) Peter   (c) Jesus
10. What prophet described the Lord as tossing up a person like a <u>ball</u>?
    (a) Jeremiah   (b) Isaiah   (c) Zechariah

60. Pillars

1. Who set up a pillar as a self monument because he had no son to erect such a stone to his memory?
2. Who set up a pillar to mark his wife's grave?
3. What blind man pulled down pillars of a temple, killing himself and thousands of heathen worshipers?
4. Who had a porch of pillars constructed for his new home?
5. Who was made king of Israel by the "pillar that was in Shechem"?
6. Who built an altar, surrounded by twelve pillars, at the foot of a hill?
7. What was the name given to the two metal pillars that stood at the main entrance of Solomon's temple?
8. What three apostles did Paul liken to pillars?
9. Who said a pillar of stone would be a witness of vows taken between himself and his son-in-law?
10. What prophet was told by God that he would make an iron pillar?

61. Precious Stones

Unscramble the scrambled word in each sentence to discover a precious stone.

1. "There was a rainbow round about the throne, in sight like unto an LEEMDRA."
2. "And I will make thy windows of GAASTE."
3. "The POATZ of Ethiopia shall not equal it."
4. "His body also was like the YLERB."
5. "The sin of Judah is written with a pen of iron, and with the point of a AIDNODM."
6. "The likeness of a throne, as the appearance of a IASRHPPE stone."
7. "The gold of that land is good: there is bdellium and the XNOY stone."
8. "No mention shall be made of CLRAO."
9. "A virtuous woman . . . her price is far above REBIUS."
10. "The building of the wall of it was of SRAJPE."

62. Proverb Things

Numerous things are mentioned in Solomon's Proverbs. Unscramble the letters to discover these items.

1. "The hoary head is a RNWOC of glory. . . ."
2. "Wisdom is better than SUIBER. . . ."
3. "Better is a dinner of BREHS where love is, than a stalled ox and hatred therewith."
4. ". . . ERADB eaten in secret is pleasant."
5. "A word fitly spoken is like LEPASP of gold in pictures of silver."
6. "Burning lips and a wicked heart are like a EOPRHSTD covered with silver dross."
7. "Every word of God is pure: he is a HLEISD unto them that put their trust in him."
8. "Better is a dry ERLOSM, and quietness therewith, than an house full of sacrifices with strife."
9. "A merry heart doeth good like a ICEIDNEM. . . ."
10. "For there shall be no reward . . . the CNLADE of the wicked shall be put out."

63. They Rent Their Clothes

The Scripture people, listed at the left, tore their clothing to express grief or distress over a situation. The situations are listed at the right. See if you can match them.

1. Reuben
2. Jephthah
3. David
4. Barnabas
5. Ezra
6. Elisha
7. Job
8. Mordecai
9. Athaliah
10. Josiah

a. When hearing the words of the book of the law read.
b. When a dear friend was carried up to heaven.
c. When hearing a king's decree that all Jews were to be killed.
d. When met by his daughter, knowing she was to be sacrificed.
e. When hearing of the death of all his sons and daughters.
f. On finding a brother missing from a pit.
g. When hearing people praising a newly appointed king.
h. When mistaken for a Greek god.
i. On hearing of the death of a king and his son.
j. When told of mixed marriages.

64. Revelation's Symbolism

Revelation is filled with symbolism. Hidden in the sentences are the following symbolic terms. See if you can find them.

Altar	Beast	Bride	Gate	King
Lamb	Rivers	Sea	Horns	Sun

1. Instructions to Israelites: "Covenants of meat and salt are always offered together."
2. Elijah said to Ahab, "ride in your chariot, down the mountain."
3. Because of his unbelief, Thomas has been called "doubting Thomas."
4. Jeremiah dictated to Baruch, the scribe, a stirring scroll to be read.
5. Eve, because of the serpent's beguiling, ate of the forbidden fruit.
6. To Ezekiel, amber was a bright color.
7. People were making sounds of joy when Solomon was anointed.
8. Pharoah's chariot drivers pursued the Israelites into the sea.
9. Jethro told Moses to appoint men to judge at all seasons.
10. After his hair was shorn, Samson lost his strength.

65. Rings

1. Who had a ring placed on his finger by his father?
2. Who had a king's ring placed on his finger to be worn as a badge of authority?
3. To what building were rings brought to be included among "an offering of gold unto the LORD"?
4. Who said a fair woman without discretion is like a gold ring in a pig's snout?
5. What prophet foretold of God taking away the rings of prideful women?
6. What king sealed the mouth of a lions' den with his signet ring?
7. What apostle mentioned a man entering a church wearing fine clothes and a gold ring?
8. Who did Jeremiah say this about, "though . . . the son of Jehoiakim . . . were the signet upon my right hand, yet I pluck thee hence"?
9. Who had a king's ring given to him and then had it taken away?
10. Who was then given Ahasuerus's ring?

66. Royal Apparel

1. What ruler after putting on his royal robes sat on his throne, and made a speech to delegates from Tyre and Sidon?
2. What king had the skirt of his robe cut off by an enemy?
3. What man when appointed prime minister by a king put on royal robes, a gold crown, and coat of linen and purple?
4. Unscramble the mixed-up words in this quotation from Psalms: "The king's daughter is all glorious within: her clothing is of UTHROGW DLGO."
5. Who requested that he be given the "purple raiment that was on the kings of Midian"?
6. What king when he heard words read from a newly found holy book tore his clothes?
7. What king's son gave his robe, sword, bow, and belt to a man he had just met?
8. According to Jesus, Solomon "in all his glory was not arrayed" like what?
9. What king, during a joyful procession, was "clothed with a robe of fine linen"?
10. What king clothed a man in scarlet robes of royal honor because he had interpreted his dream?

67. Scripture Currency

Hidden in each sentence below is a variety of Scripture currency. With the word bank to help you, see if you can find the money.

Brass	Dram	Farthing	Gerah	Maneh
Mite	Penny	Pound	Shekel	Talent

1. Jesus asked the soldier who struck him, "why smitest thou me?"
2. A left-handed man, Ehud, assassinated Eglon.
3. Paul expounded Christianity in all of his sermons.
4. God instructed Moses to use brassware in the tabernacle altar.
5. Jacob put a lentil in the pottage he served Esau.
6. Early Christians, for church services, kept their homes open. Nymphas was one of these.
7. Joshua used rams' horns to blow signals.
8. From near and far, things of value were brought to Solomon.
9. Out of anger, Ahasuerus banished Queen Vashti.
10. "Has he kelp in his haul of fish?" people wondered when Peter pulled in his net.

68. Shining Silver

Match each person at the left to his connection with the proper silver item or items, listed at the right.

1. Ephraim
2. Moses
3. Joseph
4. Demetrius
5. David
6. Ahasuerus
7. Joram
8. Abraham's servant
9. Solomon
10. Isaiah

a. He had beds made of silver.
b. This traveler gave a girl silver jewels.
c. He made silver shrines for the Greek goddess Diana.
d. He uses the analogy of apples of gold in pictures of silver.
e. He brought silver vessels as gifts for David.
f. He said the goldsmith casteth silver chains.
g. God instructed him to make two silver trumpets.
h. He ordered a silver cup to be hidden in a grain sack.
i. He said, "yet shall ye be as the wings of a dove covered with silver. . . ."
j. He stole 1,100 shekels of silver from his mother.

69. Ships' Parts

Each word in the following word bank is part of a ship of Scripture times. Can you find them hidden in the sentences?

        Anchor   Boat   Forepart   Helm
        Mast   Oar   Sail   Side

1. "My servant is ailing," the centurion told Jesus.
2. Before parting, David and Jonathan made a covenant with each other.
3. Absalom's hair caught in the branch, or strong limb, of an oak.
4. Simon, the tanner, resided in a house by the sea.
5. After a confab, oaths were exchanged between Abraham and Abimelech.
6. David said, "Horror hath overwhelmed me."
7. Moses was told to array Aaron in special clothing.
8. Speaking of Jesus, Peter described Him as the chief cornerstone.

70. Shoes

Match the persons at the left to the correct reference to a shoe, listed at the right.

1. Abraham
2. Peter
3. Joshua
4. David
5. John the Baptist
6. Asher
7. Boaz
8. Moses
9. Ezekiel
10. Amos

a. He took off his shoe to bind a contract.
b. God told him, "put off thy shoes from off thy feet."
c. Moses foretold his shoes would be of iron and brass.
d. An angel told him to put on his sandals.
e. He said, "They sold . . . the poor for a pair of shoes."
f. He mentioned shoes being made of badger skin.
g. He refused to take a shoe latchet from the king of Sodom.
h. An angel with a drawn sword told him, "Loose thy shoe from off thy foot."
i. He said he was not worthy to unloose Jesus' shoe latchets.
j. This mourner climbed a mountain without his shoes.

71. Shut the Door

1. Who shut the door of Noah's Ark?
2. How many tardy bridesmaids found the door shut to them at a wedding?
3. Who were meeting behind shut doors when the resurrected Jesus appeared among them?
4. Who advised going into a closet, shutting its door, and then praying?
5. What did the man in Jesus' illustration refuse to do after he had shut his door and gone to bed?
6. Who told a widow to go inside, shut the door, and pour olive oil into pans?
7. Who, after being dragged out of a temple, had its doors shut behind him?
8. What prophet said, "Who is there even among you that would shut the doors for nought?"
9. What man shut a door behind him and went outside to speak to a mob?
10. Who, even though in danger of being killed, refused to go in and then shut temple doors?

72. The Sound of Music

Each quotation below contains the name of a musical instrument used in Biblical times. Only the first letter of each instrument is given. Your task is to fill in the remaining letters.

1. "And Jephthah came to Mizpeh . . . and, behold, his daughter came out to meet him with T_____. . . ."
2. "Asaph made a sound with C_____."
3. "With trumpets and sound of C_____ make a joyful noise before the Lord, the King."
4. ". . . when the evil spirit from God was upon Saul . . . David took an H_____. . . ."
5. "Jubal: he was the father of all such as handle the harp and O_____."
6. ". . . when all the people heard the sound of the cornet, flute, harp, S_____, psaltery . . . all the people . . . fell down and worshipped the golden image that Nebuchadnezzar the king had set up."
7. "That chant to the sound of the V_____, and invent to themselves instruments of musick, like David."
8. ". . . the women came out of all cities of Israel, singing and dancing, to meet king Saul, with T_____. . . ."
9. ". . . when thou art come thither to the city . . . thou shalt meet a company of prophets coming down from the high place with a P_____. . . ."
10. "And there happened to be a man of Belial, whose name was Sheba . . . and he blew a T_____. . . ."

73. The Sound of Trumpets

1. Who was instructed to make two silver trumpets?
2. What king was serenaded with a trumpet at his coronation?
3. What happened when Gideon's trumpets sounded?
4. How many priests blew trumpets during the induction ceremony of the ark?
5. What queen tore her clothes and screamed, "Treason, Treason," at the sound of trumpets?
6. How many priests blew trumpets and marched around the walls of Jericho?
7. What man blew a trumpet and then revolted against David?
8. Who foretold that a trumpet would be used to waken the dead?
9. What escaped murderer blew a trumpet in the mountain of Ephraim as a call to arms and mustered an army?
10. Who blew a trumpet to signal his army to stop the pursuit of the Israelites?

74. Sticks and Stones

1. What boy carried sticks of wood with which he was to be burned?
2. Who took five stones out of a brook?
3. Whose wooden staff sprouted and blossomed?
4. Who set up twelve stones in the middle of a river?
5. Who put rods of wood in watering troughs?
6. Who used many stones in the construction of his house?
7. Whose rod turned into a serpent?
8. What prophet was told to hide stones in a brick kiln?
9. Who had his lunch touched by an angel's staff and consumed by fire?
10. Who set up a stone and called it Ebenezer?

75. Sweet Incense

1. Who were destroyed by fire because they unlawfully offered incense before God?
2. What prophet had a vision of seventy men, each holding a censer of burning incense?
3. Who was burning incense in a temple when an angel appeared and told him his wife would have a baby?
4. How often was incense to be burned on the tabernacle altar?
5. Who was stricken with leprosy because he offered forbidden incense?
6. How did the princes carry their offering of incense to the dedication of the altar?
7. Who used incense to stop a plague?
8. Who angered God by building temples for his wives to use for burning incense and sacrificing to idols?
9. Who had a vision of an angel holding a golden censer with a great quantity of incense?
10. Who was given a recipe by God for making incense?

76. Swords

Match each person at the left to his association with a sword, listed at the right.

1. Eleazar
2. Jonathan
3. Peter
4. Joshua
5. Ahimelech
6. Joab
7. David
8. Goliath
9. Saul
10. Esau

a. He was told by his father "by thy sword shalt thou live. . . ."
b. He saw an angel stand between earth and heaven holding a sword.
c. He smote Philistines "until his hand clave unto the sword."
d. When badly wounded in battle he committed suicide by falling on a sword.
e. He gave a beloved friend his sword.
f. He "discomfited Amalek and his people with the edge of the sword."
g. He cut off a servant's ear with his sword.
h. While pretending to kiss a man, he murdered him with his sword.
i. He gave David Goliath's sword.
j. He had his head cut off with his own sword.

77. Tabernacle Furnishings

Hidden in each of the sentences below is a tabernacle furnishing. Use the word bank to help you discover these hidden items.

    Altar   Ark   Bason   Bowls   Dish
    Hanging   Laver   Table   Tent   Veil

1. Ahab, a son of Omri, was a wicked king.
2. In a song, David said, "By God have I leaped over a wall."
3. Saul, a very angry man, tried to kill David.
4. In the book of Job, owls are mentioned.
5. Nabal tartly refused David's request for food.
6. The discontented Israelites complained and thus displeased God.
7. Paul said, "Have renounced the hidden things of dishonesty."
8. There was darkness in all the land of Egypt.
9. Ahasuerus ordered, "Let Haman hang in gallows he prepared for another man."
10. Moses was told by Jethro that he alone was not able to counsel Israelites.

78. Tables

1. What king fed seventy kings under his table with scraps of food?
2. Who was instructed to make a table of shittim wood for a temple?
3. Who put a table in a guest room prepared for a prophet?
4. Who asked, "Can God furnish a table in the wilderness?"
5. Who overthrew the moneychangers' tables?
6. Who had a gold table made for a temple?
7. What man, who had been raised from the dead, sat at a table with Jesus?
8. Who was told he was to eat bread "continually" at David's table?
9. Who arose from his father's table in anger?
10. Who regularly fed 150 Jewish officials at his table?

79. Talents

1. Who hired 100,000 experienced mercenaries for one hundred silver talents?
2. Who bought the hill, Samaria, for two talents of silver?
3. What servant, because he took a present of two talents of silver, was punished with leprosy?
4. Who took the king of Rabbah's crown that weighed a talent of gold and placed it on his head?
5. In Jesus' parable of the talents, how many talents did a servant hide in the ground?
6. What king paid a heavy tribute of three hundred talents of silver and thirty talents of gold to the king of Assyria?
7. What king was given expensive gifts by a queen that included twenty talents of gold?
8. What prophet saw a talent of lead?
9. Who offered to pay 10,000 talents of silver into a king's treasury to cover expenses for purging Jews?
10. Who had a vision of hailstones that weighed about a talent each?

80. The Tender Grape

1. Who was attacked by a lion in a vineyard?
2. Who sang about grapes of gall and bitter clusters?
3. Who planted the first vineyard?
4. What was the Hebrew law concerning grapes?
5. Who had a vision of an angel with a sickle cutting off clusters of grapes?
6. At what place did spies cut down a cluster of grapes?
7. Who washed his clothes in the "blood of grapes"?
8. Who interpreted a dream about grapes?
9. Who refused to give his vineyard to a king?
10. What two prophets mentioned fathers eating sour grapes?

81. Tents

Match the persons at the left to their connection with a tent, listed at the right.

1. Achan
2. Jabal
3. Abraham
4. Laban
5. Sisera
6. Aquila
7. Gideon
8. Isaac
9. David
10. Moses

a. Searched a tent for stolen household idols.
b. Overheard a dream about barley bread flattening a tent.
c. Stored a slain giant's armor in his tent.
d. Hid battle spoils under his tent.
e. Was "father of all such as dwell in tents."
f. Took his father-in-law into his tent for a talk.
g. Sat in a tent door during the heat of day.
h. Was murdered in a woman's tent.
i. Pitched his tent in the Valley of Gerar.
j. Was a tentmaker.

82. Thorns and Briers

1. Who wore a "crown of thorns"?
2. Who used thorns and briers to punish men who had refused to give bread to his army?
3. Who was instructed by God to drive out Canaanites or they would become thorns in the side?
4. In which of Jesus' parables did he mention thorns?
5. Who said, "The way of the slothful man is as an hedge of thorns"?
6. What prophet was told that wicked people had sown wheat, but would reap thorns because God was angry with them?
7. Who was punished by having thorns and thistles as his crops?
8. Who saw a man in a vision who told him not to be afraid of briers and thorns?
9. Who talks about brambles in a fable?
10. What prophet foretold that thorns would come up in palaces, and nettles and brambles in fortresses?

83. Thrones

1. Who had an ivory throne overlaid with gold?
2. Who, in a vision, saw a rainbow around a throne?
3. How many thrones did Jesus promise to his disciples?
4. Who had his throne set upon stones and hidden in a brick kiln?
5. What throne did the angel tell Mary her son would receive from God?
6. What prophet said the city of Jerusalem would be known as the throne of the Lord?
7. What mother had a throne placed beside that of her royal son?
8. Who had a vision of the "Ancient of days" sitting upon a fiery throne, brought in on flaming wheels?
9. Who, after making a speech to the people from his throne, was stricken with a horrible sickness?
10. What two kings sat on thrones placed at the entrance of Samaria's gates with prophets prophesying before them?

84. "Thy Rod and Thy Staff"

1. Who armed with only a shepherd's staff and sling faced up to a formidable foe?
2. Who gave the names Beauty and Bands to two staffs?
3. How many rods did Moses put in the inner room of the tabernacle?
4. Who said he passed over Jordan with his staff?
5. Who dipped the end of a rod into a honeycomb?
6. Who was told to lay a staff on a child's face?
7. Whose rod turned into a serpent?
8. Whose lunch was touched by an angel's staff and then consumed by fire?
9. Whose wooden rod budded and blossomed?
10. Who said, "thy rod and thy staff they comfort me"?

85. Treasure Hunt

Using the word bank, choose the correct word, or group of words, needed to fill the blanks below.

Crown   Gold chain   Gold earring
Gold, frankincense, and myrrh   Golden calf   Pearl
Silver and gold   Spices, gold, and precious stones
Twelve precious stones   Two bracelets

1. Aaron made a _____ from earrings.
2. Abraham was very rich in cattle, _____.
3. Each of Job's friends gave him a _____.
4. Daniel was given a _____ by King Belshazzar.
5. The queen of Sheba brought Solomon gifts of _____.
6. Rebekah was given _____ by Abraham's servant.
7. King Ahasuerus gave Esther a _____.
8. The breastplate of the high priest of the tabernacle was adorned with _____.
9. The merchant in Jesus' parable found a _____.
10. The wise men brought gifts of _____ to the baby Jesus.

86. Trees

Each Bible person at the left had an association with a tree, listed at the right. See if you can match them.

1. David
2. Zacchaeus
3. Deborah
4. Absalom
5. Saul
6. Hiram
7. Nathanael
8. Baal-hanan
9. Elijah
10. Solomon

a. Was hung in an oak.
b. Was under a fig tree when seen by Jesus.
c. Sat under a juniper tree and prayed to die.
d. Listened for sounds in mulberry trees.
e. Climbed a sycamore tree.
f. Used algum trees to make harps and lutes.
g. Dwelt under a palm tree.
h. He and his soldiers camped by a pomegranate tree.
i. Had charge of David's olive trees.
j. Furnished fir trees for temple construction.

87. Veils

1. When did Moses put a veil on his face?
2. In Moses' tabernacle what did a veil separate?
3. Who, of Aaron's descendants, were forbidden to go behind the tabernacle veil?
4. When the Israelites moved their camp what was Aaron to do with the tabernacle veil?
5. What material was used for the veil in Solomon's temple?
6. Which newly engaged girl covered her face with a veil when about to meet her fiancé?
7. Who measured six measures of barley into a woman's veil?
8. What prophet warned that vain women, wearing veils, would have them taken by God?
9. On what occasion was a temple veil torn from top to bottom?
10. Who used a veil as a symbolic token of spiritual blindness?

88. Windows

1. What wicked queen was thrown out of a window to her death?
2. What mother watched from a window for her son's return?
3. Who hung a scarlet cord from a window?
4. Who released a raven from a window?
5. Who looked out of a window of his house and saw "a young man void of understanding"?
6. Following the instructions of an ill prophet, what king opened a window and shot an arrow from it?
7. Who prayed three times a day in front of open windows?
8. What wanted man made his escape by being let down through a window in a basket?
9. Who fell asleep on a window sill and tumbled out, landing three stories below?
10. What woman, watching from a window, was disgusted at the sight of her husband leaping and dancing?

89. Wood

Match each person at the left with his particular tie-in with wood, listed at the right.

1. David
2. Aaron
3. Jacob
4. Solomon
5. Noah
6. Bezaleel
7. Ezra
8. Isaac
9. Jeremiah
10. Ornan

a. Made a tabernacle table of shittim wood.
b. Carried wood with which he was to be burned as an offering.
c. Used wood to decorate a palace.
d. Wore a wooden yoke on his neck.
e. Stood on a wooden stand and read a scroll of Moses' law.
f. Gave wooden threshing instruments to be used as fuel for a burnt offering.
g. Had a wooden rod that blossomed.
h. Placed wooden rods beside watering troughs.
i. Used gopher wood to build a boat.
j. Played an instrument made of fir wood.

90. What Became of These?

What became of each of the following Scripture articles?

1. Joseph's coat of many colors
2. Noah's ark
3. Jesus' seamless coat
4. Moses' bronze serpent
5. Elijah's mantle
6. Israelites' manna
7. Solomon's temple
8. Goliath's sword
9. Judas's thirty pieces of silver
10. Aaron's golden calf

ANSWERS

1. Ark of the Covenant

1. Bezaleel (Exod. 37:1)
2. Shittim wood (Exod. 37:1)
3. Golden jar containing manna, Aaron's staff that budded, stone tablets with the Ten Commandments (Heb. 9:4)
4. Joshua (Josh. 3:5-17)
5. Philistines (I Sam. 4:10-11)
6. Uzzah (II Sam. 6:6-7)
7. Obededom (II Sam. 6:10-11)
8. David (II Sam. 6:12-15)
9. Tent (I Chron. 15:1)
10. Levites (I Chron. 15:2)

2. Assemble the Ensemble

1. (a) long (Mark 12:38)
2. (b) purple (Mark 15:17)
3. (b) divers (II Sam. 13:18)
4. (b) borders (Matt. 23:5)
5. (a) best (Luke 15:22)
6. (a) gay (James 2:3)
7. (c) gold (Ps. 45:13)
8. (c) soft (Luke 7:25)
9. (c) linen (Jer. 13:1)
10. (b) tapestry (Prov. 31:22)

3. Axes

1. Solomon's temple (I Kings 6:7)
2. Abimelech (Judg. 9:48)
3. David (I Chron. 20:1-3)
4. John the Baptist (Matt. 3:10)
5. Asaph (Ps. 74:5)
6. Elisha (II Kings 6:5-6)
7. City of Refuge (Deut. 19:5)
8. Israelites (Deut. 20:19)
9. Ezekiel (Ezek. 26:9)
10. To the Philistines (I Sam. 13:20)

4. Baked Goods

1. Ten (Lev. 26:26)
2. Pharaoh's chief baker (Gen. 40:16-17)
3. Lot (Gen. 19:1, 3)
4. Tamar (II Sam. 13:8)
5. Elijah (I Kings 19:5-6)
6. Manna (Num. 11:7-8)
7. Jeremiah (Jer. 37:21)
8. Abraham (Gen. 18:2, 6)
9. Levites (I Chron. 23:27-29)
10. Samuel (I Sam. 8:10, 13)

5. Barley

1. f (Rev. 6:6)
2. i (Exod. 9:22-23, 31)
3. j (Hos. 3:1-2)
4. a (Judg. 7:13)
5. h (II Sam. 14:30)
6. g (II Kings 4:42-44)
7. e (Ruth 3:2)
8. b (Ezek. 4:9-12)
9. d (I Kings 4:26, 28)
10. c (II Sam. 21:8-9)

6. Baskets

1. Gideon (Judg. 6:19-20)
2. Saul (Acts 9:24-25)
3. Amos (Amos 8:1-2)
4. Pharaoh's chief baker (Gen. 40:16)
5. Moses (Deut. 28:5, 17)
6. Aaron (Exod. 29:1-3)
7. Jezreel (II Kings 10:7-8)
8. Jeremiah (Jer. 24:1)
9. Seven (Mark 8:1-9)
10. Twelve (Matt. 14:19-21)

7. Beds

1. f (Deut. 3:11)
2. i (Matt. 9:6)
3. j (II Kings 4:10)
4. a (II Sam. 4:5–7)
5. h (Isa. 28:20)
6. g (II Kings 1:2–4)
7. e (Esther 1:1, 6)
8. b (Exod. 8:1, 3)
9. d (I Sam. 19:11–16)
10. c (I Sam. 28:20–23)

8. Bible Plants

1. Mandrakes (Gen. 30:14)
2. Thistles & cockle (Job 31:40)
3. Gourd (Jonah 4:6)
4. Lily (Luke 12:27)
5. Rose (Isa. 35:1)
6. Hyssop (John 19:29)
7. Nettles (Prov. 24:30–31)
8. Mint & Rue (Luke 11:42)
9. Bulrushes (Exod. 2:2–3)
10. Coriander (Exod. 16:31)

9. Boats

1. e (Jonah 1:4–5)
2. d (II Sam. 19:18)
3. b (Gen. 6:14–16)
4. j (I Kings 22:48)
5. g (I Kings 9:26)
6. i (Luke 5:1–3)
7. f (Acts 27:41)
8. c (Mark 1:19–20)
9. a (Isa. 18:2)
10. h (Gen. 49:13)

10. Book Report

1. j (II Kings 22:1, 10–11)
2. g (Neh. 8:1–5)
3. h (Jer. 51:60–63)
4. c (Job 31:35)
5. i (Jer. 36:9, 23)
6. a (Esther 6:1)
7. e (Josh. 18:8–9)
8. b (Exod. 32:32)
9. d (Acts 19:1, 19)
10. f (Ezek. 3:1–3)

11. Bottles and Cruses

1. Elisha (II Kings 2:19–22)
2. Jael (Judg. 4:18–19)
3. Job (Job 38:37)
4. Elijah (I Kings 19:5–6)
5. Jeremiah (Jer. 19:1, 10)
6. Jesus (Matt. 9:17)
7. Jeroboam (I Kings 14:2–3)
8. Ziba (II Sam. 16:1)
9. David (Ps. 56:8)
10. Abraham (Gen. 21:14)

12. Bows and Arrows

1. e (Gen. 27:3)
2. j (I Sam. 31:2–4)
3. b (Gen. 21:20)
4. f (II Kings 13:14–19)
5. g (I Sam. 20:20–22)
6. h (Jer. 50:14)
7. i (I Kings 22:34–35)
8. d (Job 6:4)
9. c (II Chron. 35:22–23)
10. a (II Sam. 22:15)

13. Brass

1. Moses (Num. 21:9)
2. Apostles (Matt. 10:9)
3. Zechariah (Zech. 6:1)
4. Paul (I Cor. 13:1)
5. Goliath (I Sam. 17:4–5)
6. Samson (Judg. 16:21)
7. Rehoboam (II Chron. 12:9–10)
8. Hiram (I Kings 7:13–15)
9. Job (Job 6:12)
10. Nebuchadnezzar (Dan. 2:1, 31–32)

14. Bread

1. c (I Kings 17:6)
2. h (I Kings 18:4)
3. j (Gen. 47:17)
4. g (Ezek. 4:9–12)
5. f (Jer. 37:21)
6. i (Judg. 7:13)
7. e (Exod. 16:4)
8. a (Gen. 19:1–3)
9. b (Gen. 31:54)
10. d (II Kings 4:8)

15. Breakage

1. f (Exod. 32:15, 19)
2. d (II Kings 23:12–15)
3. i (Judg. 7:19)
4. h (II Kings 18:1, 4)
5. j (Mark 14:3)
6. b (Judg. 16:9)
7. e (Acts 27:35)
8. c (Mark 2:1, 4)
9. g (Exod. 32:2–3)
10. a (Gen. 19:4, 9)

16. Cakes

1. Hosea (Hosea 7:8)
2. Israelites (Lev. 24:5)
3. Elijah (I Kings 17:10, 13)
4. Abraham (Gen. 18:6)
5. Aaron (Exod. 29:23–24)
6. Abigail (I Sam. 25:18, 32–35)
7. Fresh oil (Num. 11:8)
8. Jeremiah (Jer. 7:18)
9. David (I Sam. 30:11–12)
10. Gideon (Judg. 7:13)

17. Candles and Candlesticks

1. Bezaleel (Exod. 37:1, 17)
2. Elisha (II Kings 4:10)
3. Ten (II Chron. 4:7)
4. Belshazzar (Dan. 5:1, 5)
5. Two (Rev. 11:4)
6. Under a bushel (Matt. 5:15)
7. Jerusalem (Zeph. 1:12)
8. Job (Job 29:3)
9. David (Ps. 18:28)
10. Piece of silver (Luke 15:8)

18. Cedar

1. David (II Sam. 7:2)
2. Priest (Lev. 14:48–49)
3. Jotham (Judg. 9:7, 15)
4. Lebanon (Ps. 92:12)
5. Isaiah (Isa. 41:19)
6. Jehoash (II Kings 14:8–9)
7. Solomon (Song of Sol. 4:11)
8. Ezekiel (Ezek. 27:5)
9. Hiram (II Sam. 5:11; I Kings 5:2, 6)
10. Balaam (Num. 24:1–6)

19. Chariots

1. i (II Kings 9:20)
2. e (Judg. 4:2–3)
3. f (I Kings 22:34–35)
4. g (II Kings 5:21)
5. d (I Chron. 19:6–7)
6. c (Gen. 46:29)
7. a (Exod. 14:7, 28)
8. j (II Kings 2:11)
9. b (I Kings 9:19)
10. h (Acts 8:27–28)

20. Coats

1. Samuel (I Sam. 2:18–19)
2. Let him have the cloak also (Matt. 5:40)
3. Dorcas (Acts 9:36–40)
4. With embroidery (Exod. 28:4)
5. Two (Matt. 10:10)
6. Joseph (Gen. 37:3–4)
7. John the Baptist (Luke 3:11)
8. Jesus (John 19:23)
9. Shadrach, Meshach, Abednego (Dan. 3:20–21)
10. Skins (Gen. 3:21)

21. The Color Red

1. j (Dan. 5:7, 16, 29)
2. a (Josh. 2:1, 18, 21)
3. g (Jer. 22:14)
4. b (Num. 19:2–3)
5. e (Gen. 25:25)
6. c (Matt. 27:27–28)
7. d (Rev. 12:3)
8. f (Gen. 49:10, 12)
9. h (Gen. 25:30)
10. i (Zech. 1:8)

22. Commercial Articles

1. Apes (I Kings 10:22)
2. Balm (Gen. 37:25)
3. Gold (I Kings 10:22)
4. Honey (Ezek. 27:17)
5. Horse (I Kings 10:25)
6. Iron (Ezek. 27:12)
7. Linen (Rev. 18:12)
8. Oil (Ezek. 27:17)
9. Wheat (Rev. 18:13)
10. Wine (Ezek. 27:18)

23. Cooking Equipment

1. Dish (II Kings 21:13)
2. Pot (Judg. 6:19)
3. Platter (Matt. 23:25)
4. Bowl (Judg. 6:38)
5. Pan (Lev. 6:21)
6. Pitcher (Luke 22:10)
7. Cup (Gen. 40:11)
8. Bason (Exod. 27:3)
9. Oven (Lev. 26:26)
10. Sieve (Amos 9:9)

24. Cords and Ropes

1. Jesus (John 2:15)
2. Micah (Micah 2:5)
3. Delilah (Judg. 16:12)
4. Job (Job 41:1)
5. Jeremiah (Jer. 38:6)
6. Paul (Acts 27:32)
7. Ahasuerus (Esther 1:6)
8. Rahab (Josh. 2:1, 15)
9. Benhadad (I Kings 20:32)
10. Solomon (Eccles. 4:12)

25. Crowns

1. John (Rev. 4:4)
2. Vashti (Esther 1:10–11)
3. Paul (II Tim. 4:8)
4. Joash (II Kings 11:4–12)
5. Zechariah (Zech. 6:10–11)
6. Aaron (Exod. 28:36–38)
7. Solomon (Song of Sol. 3:11)
8. Ezekiel (Ezek. 21:25–26)
9. Saul (II Sam. 1:10)
10. David (II Sam. 12:30)

26. Cups

1. Golden (Jer. 51:7)
2. Salvation (Ps. 116:13)
3. Consolation (Jer. 16:7)
4. Blessing (I Cor. 10:16)
5. Astonishment (Ezek. 23:33)
6. Fury (Isa. 51:17)
7. Devils (I Cor. 10:21)
8. Trembling (Zech. 12:2)
9. Water (Mark 9:41)
10. Indignation (Rev. 14:10)

27. Ephods

1. Aaron (Exod. 28:3–4)
2. Blue (Exod. 28:31)
3. Names of the twelve tribes of Israel (Exod. 28:9)
4. Bezaleel (Exod. 37:1; 39:2)
5. Gideon (Judg. 8:22–27)
6. Micah (Judg. 18:13–17)
7. Samuel (I Sam. 2:18)
8. Abiathar (I Sam. 30:7–8)
9. Doeg (I Sam. 22:18)
10. David (II Sam. 6:14)

28. Figs

1. Isaiah (II Kings 20:7)
2. Adam & Eve (Gen. 3:7)
3. Jesus (Mark 11:11, 13)
4. Jeremiah (Jer. 24:1)
5. Abigail (I Sam. 25:18)
6. Jotham (Judg. 9:7, 10)
7. Nehemiah (Neh. 13:15)
8. Egyptian (I Sam. 30:11–12)
9. Nathanael (John 1:48)
10. Moses' spies (Num. 13:2, 23)

29. Favored with Gifts

1. g (Gen. 32:1, 13–15)
2. d (I Kings 14:2–3)
3. h (Gen. 45:21–22)
4. j (Josh. 15:17–19)
5. i (I Kings 15:18–19)
6. c (II Chron. 9:9)
7. a (Gen. 24:2, 15–22)
8. b (I Kings 9:12)
9. f (Matt. 2:1, 11)
10. e (I Sam. 18:4)

30. Fiery Furnaces

1. Abraham (Gen. 15:12, 17)
2. Nebuchadnezzar (Dan. 3:1–6)
3. Ezekiel (Ezek. 22:22)
4. Mount Sinai (Exod. 19:18)
5. David (Ps. 21:9)
6. Sodom & Gomorrah (Gen. 19:28)
7. Shadrach, Meshach, Abednego (Dan. 3:20)
8. Parable of the Tares (Matt. 13:24–30, 41–42)
9. Moses (Exod. 9:8)
10. Nehemiah (Neh. 12:27, 38)

31. Fruit

1. Ahab (I Kings 21:1-2)
2. David (I Sam. 30:11-12)
3. Joel (Joel 1:4, 12)
4. Jesus (Matt. 21:18-19)
5. Noah (Gen. 9:20)
6. Eve (Gen. 3:1-6)
7. Pomegranate (Exod. 28:33)
8. Joseph (Gen. 40:9-13)
9. Israelites (Num. 11:5)
10. Abigail (I Sam. 25:18)

32. Get the Point?

1. c (I Sam. 18:11)
2. e (Judg. 3:31)
3. g (Jer. 36:23)
4. f (Judg. 4:21)
5. i (II Sam. 18:14)
6. h (I Chron. 11:23-24)
7. b (Gen. 22:6)
8. j (II Kings 9:24)
9. d (Judg. 3:16)
10. a (John 18:10)

33. The Golden Corn

1. f (I Sam. 17:17)
2. i (Ruth 2:14)
3. j (Gen. 42:1-2)
4. a (Matt. 12:1)
5. h (II Sam. 17:19)
6. g (Gen. 41:1, 5)
7. e (Judg. 15:5-6)
8. b (Gen. 41:49)
9. d (Josh. 5:11)
10. c (II Kings 4:42)

34. Golden Possessions

1. d (Dan. 3:1)
2. e (I Kings 12:26-28)
3. a (I Chron. 20:2)
4. b (Esther 1:1, 6)
5. i (I Kings 14:25-26)
6. j (Judg. 8:24-27)
7. g (Exod. 28:30, 33)
8. f (Job 42:10-11)
9. h (Dan. 5:29)
10. c (II Chron. 4:8)

35. Grains

1. Ornan (I Chron. 21:20)
2. Absalom (II Sam. 14:30)
3. Gideon (Judg. 6:11)
4. Flax & Barley (Exod. 9:24, 31)
5. Simon Peter (Luke 22:31)
6. Flax (Josh. 2:6)
7. Samson (Judg. 15:4)
8. Boaz (Ruth 3:2)
9. Isaac (Gen. 26:12)
10. Samuel (I Sam. 12:17-18)

36. Grains of Salt

1. Elisha (II Kings 2:19-22)
2. Disciples (Matt. 5:13)
3. Job (Job 6:6)
4. Abimelech (Judg. 9:41-45)
5. Amaziah (II Chron. 25:11)
6. David (II Chron. 13:5)
7. Ezekiel (Ezek. 16:4)
8. Lot's wife (Gen. 19:23-26)
9. Jesus (Mark 9:49)
10. Meat offerings (Lev. 2:13)

37. Grass

1. Third (Gen. 1:11–13)
2. Ahab & Obadiah (I Kings 18:5–6)
3. Job (Job 40:15)
4. Nebuchadnezzar (Dan. 4:25, 33)
5. David (Ps. 129:6)
6. John (Rev. 8:7)
7. About 5,000 (Matt. 14:19–21)
8. Jesus (Luke 12:28)
9. Israelites (Deut. 11:15)
10. Amos (Amos 7:1–2)

38. Honey and the Honeycomb

1. Ahijah (I Kings 14:2, 4)
2. Samson (Judg. 14:8–9)
3. Jonathan (I Sam. 14:27, 43–45)
4. Jesus (Luke 24:36, 41–43)
5. Jacob (Deut. 32:9, 13)
6. John the Baptist (Matt. 3:4)
7. Canaan (Exod. 3:8, 17)
8. Solomon (Prov. 25:27)
9. Ezekiel (Ezek. 3:1–3)
10. Israel (Gen. 43:11, 15)

39. Idol Worship

1. f (Dan. 3:1)
2. d (Exod. 32:2–4)
3. i (Gen. 31:19)
4. h (II Kings 18:1, 4)
5. j (II Chron. 15:16)
6. b (Judg. 18:17–18)
7. e (I Kings 12:28–29)
8. c (II Chron. 28:1–3)
9. g (Num. 33:52)
10. a (Gen. 35:2)

40. In the Bag

1. Naaman (II Kings 5:23)
2. Benjamin (Gen. 44:2, 12)
3. David (I Sam. 17:39–40)
4. Haggai (Hag. 1:6)
5. Disciples (Luke 12:33)
6. Isaiah (Isa. 46:6)
7. Israelites (Deut. 25:13)
8. Job (Job 14:17)
9. Judas Iscariot (John 12:4–6)
10. Gibeonites (Josh. 9:3–5)

41. In Great Abundance

1. j (I Kings 10:10)
2. g (Neh. 9:25)
3. h (II Chron. 4:18)
4. c (Ezek. 26:7, 10)
5. i (I Chron. 22:3)
6. a (II Chron. 18:2)
7. e (II Chron. 17:5)
8. b (Esther 1:1, 7)
9. d (II Chron. 2:3, 9)
10. f (II Chron. 32:29)

42. Jesus' Symbolism

1. Bread (John 6:41)
2. Star (Rev. 22:16)
3. Lion (Rev. 5:5)
4. Door (John 10:9)
5. Branch (Zech. 6:12)
6. Stone (Matt. 21:42)
7. Rock (I Cor. 10:4)
8. Root (Isa. 53:2)
9. Vine (John 15:5)
10. Lamb (John 1:29)

43. Jewelry Display

1. j (Exod. 32:2–4)
2. g (II Sam. 1:9–10)
3. h (Gen. 24:45–57)
4. c (Isa. 3:16, 18–21)
5. i (Dan. 5:7, 29)
6. a (Judg. 8:24–26)
7. e (Esther 3:10; 8:2)
8. b (I Tim. 2:9)
9. d (Gen. 35:4)
10. f (Rev. 21:19–21)

44. Kings' Things

1. c (I Kings 22:39)
2. h (Deut. 3:11)
3. j (II Kings 20:11)
4. g (Esther 5:2)
5. f (Judg. 4:13)
6. i (Dan. 3:1)
7. e (I Kings 10:18)
8. a (Jer. 36:1, 23)
9. b (I Sam. 18:10)
10. d (II Sam. 12:30)

45. Lamplight

1. Gideon (Judg. 7:15–16)
2. John (Rev. 4:5)
3. Ten (Matt. 25:1)
4. Abram (Gen. 15:9–10, 17)
5. Bezaleel (Exod. 37:1, 23)
6. David (II Sam. 22:1, 29)
7. Aaron (Num. 8:2–3)
8. Zechariah (Zech. 4:1–3)
9. Job (Job 41:1, 19)
10. Ezekiel (Ezek. 1:13)

46. The Light of the Moon

1. Joseph (Gen. 37:5, 9)
2. David (I Sam. 20:5)
3. Joshua (Josh. 10:12–13)
4. Fourth (Gen. 1:16–19)
5. Solomon (II Chron. 8:12–13)
6. Amos (Amos 8:5)
7. John (Rev. 6:12)
8. Stoned to death (Deut. 17:3–5)
9. Job (Job 31:26)
10. Josiah (II Kings 23:4–5)

47. Little Things

1. Owl (Lev. 11:17)
2. Fishes (Matt. 15:34)
3. Coat (I Sam. 2:19)
4. Book (Rev. 10:2)
5. Conies (Prov. 30:24–28)
6. Flock (Luke 12:32)
7. Chamber (Ezek. 40:7)
8. Ship (John 21:8)
9. House (Amos 6:11)
10. Lamb (II Sam. 12:3)

48. Lock and Key

1. Eglon (Judg. 3:17–25)
2. Nehemiah (Neh. 7:3)
3. Peter (Matt. 16:18–19)
4. Israelites (Deut. 3:1–5)
5. Lawyers (Luke 11:52)
6. David (Ps. 107:16)
7. John (Rev. 20:1)
8. Eliakim (Isa. 22:15–22)
9. Hanun (Neh. 3:13)
10. Twice (John 20:19, 26)

49. Lost and Found

1. Saul (I Sam. 9:3)
2. Reuben (Gen. 30:14)
3. Candle (Luke 15:8)
4. Joseph's brothers (Gen. 44:8)
5. King of Syria (I Kings 20:23, 25)
6. Samson (Judg. 15:15)
7. One (Matt. 18:12)
8. Son of a prophet (II Kings 4:38–39)
9. David (Ps. 119:176)
10. Hilkiah (II Kings 22:8)

50. Meat on the Menu

1. Ezekiel (Ezek. 24:1–5)
2. Israelites (Num. 11:13, 18–20)
3. Elisha (I Kings 19:21)
4. Prodigal son (Luke 15:13, 20–23)
5. Saul (I Sam. 28:7–8, 24–25)
6. Isaac (Gen. 27:3–4)
7. Samuel (I Sam. 9:22–24)
8. Aaron & his sons (Exod. 29:31–33)
9. Abraham (Gen. 18:2–8)

51. The Mighty Oak

1. Gideon (Judg. 6:19–20)
2. Deborah (Gen. 35:8)
3. Jacob (Gen. 35:4)
4. Amos (Amos 2:9)
5. Tyrians (Ezek. 27:2, 6)
6. Absalom (II Sam. 18:9–10)
7. Old prophet (I Kings 13:11–15)
8. Joshua (Josh. 24:25–27)
9. Saul (I Chron. 10:11–12)
10. Joash (Judg. 6:11)

52. Miraculous Foods

1. Elijah (I Kings 19:5–8)
2. Manna (Exod. 16:14–15, 35)
3. Pottage (II Kings 4:38–41)
4. Meal and oil (I Kings 17:9–16)
5. Quail (Num. 11:32)
6. Ravens (I Kings 17:6)
7. 100 (II Kings 4:42–44)
8. Gideon (Judg. 6:17–21)
9. 5,000 men, besides women and children (Matt. 14:15–21)
10. Seven (Matt. 15:32–37)

53. The Miraculous Manna

1. Because the Israelites were complaining about lack of bread (Exod. 16:2–4)
2. In the morning after the dew was gone (Exod. 16:14)
3. Hoar frost (Exod. 16:14)
4. Coriander (Exod. 16:31)
5. Wafer made with honey (Exod. 16:31)
6. In the morning (Exod. 16:12)
7. An omer (Exod. 16:16)
8. Sixth day (Exod. 16:22–23)
9. Aaron (Exod. 16:33)
10. Forty years, until they arrived at Canaan (Exod. 16:35)

54. Nests

1. Rock (Num. 24:21)
2. Stars (Obad. 4)
3. Tree (Deut. 22:6)
4. Cedars (Jer. 22:23)
5. Boughs (Ezek. 31:6)
6. Hole's mouth (Jer. 48:28)
7. Fir trees (Ps. 104:17)
8. High (Job 39:27)
9. Ground (Deut. 22:6)
10. Altars (Ps. 84:3)

55. New Things

1. i (I Kings 11:30)
2. e (Lev. 23:16)
3. f (Josh. 9:13)
4. g (Judg. 15:15–16)
5. d (Judg. 16:12)
6. c (II Sam. 6:3)
7. a (Jer. 26:10)
8. j (II Kings 2:19–20)
9. b (John 13:34)
10. h (Rev. 5:8–9)

56. Noah's Ark

1. c (Gen. 6:15)
2. b (Gen. 6:14)
3. b (Gen. 6:16)
4. b (Gen. 7:6)
5. a (Gen. 7:16)
6. c (Gen. 7:10)
7. a (Gen. 7:24)
8. c (Gen. 8:4)
9. b (Gen. 8:7)
10. a (Gen. 8:20)

57. Oil

1. Elijah (I Kings 17:10–16); Elisha (II Kings 4:1–7)
2. Hiram (I Kings 5:10–11)
3. Five (Matt. 25:1–5)
4. Good Samaritan (Luke 10:30, 33–34)
5. Rehoboam (II Chron. 11:5, 11)
6. Wise woman of Tekoah (II Sam. 14:1–2)
7. Manna (Num. 11:7–8)
8. Jacob (Gen. 28:18)
9. Moses (Exod. 30:22–25)
10. Job (Job 29:6)

58. Olive Trees

1. d (Deut. 6:10–11)
2. c (Judg. 15:4–5)
3. e (Jer. 11:16)
4. b (Luke 21:37)
5. h (I Kings 6:23, 31–33)
6. g (Ps. 52:8)
7. j (Zech. 4:1–3)
8. a (Rom. 11:17–19)
9. f (Judg. 9:7–9)
10. i (Gen. 8:10–11)

59. One and Only

1. (c) Zephaniah (Zeph. 1:12)
2. (b) Ezra (Neh. 8:3–4)
3. (a) Solomon (II Chron. 6:13)
4. (b) Jacob (Gen. 28:12)
5. (a) Jesus (Matt. 23:1, 37)
6. (c) Amos (Amos 4:2)
7. (a) Jehoiakim (Jer. 36:22–23)
8. (c) Elihu (Job 36:1; 37:18)
9. (a) Paul (Acts 19:11–12)
10. (b) Isaiah (Isa. 22:18)

60. Pillars

1. Absalom (II Sam. 18:18)
2. Jacob (Gen. 35:20)
3. Samson (Judg. 16:27–30)
4. Solomon (I Kings 7:1, 6)
5. Abimelech (Judg. 9:6)
6. Moses (Exod. 24:4)
7. Jachin & Boaz (I Kings 7:21)
8. James, Cephas, John (Gal. 2:9)
9. Laban (Gen. 31:45–52)
10. Jeremiah (Jer. 1:18)

61. Precious Stones

1. Emerald (Rev. 4:3)
2. Agates (Isa. 54:12)
3. Topaz (Job 28:19)
4. Beryl (Dan. 10:6)
5. Diamond (Jer. 17:1)
6. Sapphire (Ezek. 1:26)
7. Onyx (Gen. 2:12)
8. Coral (Job 28:18)
9. Rubies (Prov. 31:10)
10. Jasper (Rev. 21:18)

64. Revelation's Symbolism

1. Altar (Rev. 9:13)
2. Bride (Rev. 22:17)
3. Sun (Rev. 8:12)
4. Beast (Rev. 4:7)
5. Gate (Rev. 21:12)
6. Lamb (Rev. 5:6)
7. King (Rev. 1:5)
8. Rivers (Rev. 16:4)
9. Sea (Rev. 5:13)
10. Horns (Rev. 9:13)

62. Proverb Things

1. Crown (Prov. 16:31)
2. Rubies (Prov. 8:11)
3. Herbs (Prov. 15:17)
4. Bread (Prov. 9:17)
5. Apples (Prov. 25:11)
6. Potsherd (Prov. 26:23)
7. Shield (Prov. 30:5)
8. Morsel (Prov. 17:1)
9. Medicine (Prov. 17:22)
10. Candle (Prov. 24:20)

65. Rings

1. Prodigal son (Luke 15:22)
2. Joseph (Gen. 41:42)
3. Tabernacle (Exod. 35:21–22)
4. Solomon (Prov. 11:22)
5. Isaiah (Isa. 3:16, 18, 21)
6. Darius (Dan. 6:9, 16–17)
7. James (James 2:2)
8. Coniah (Jer. 22:24)
9. Haman (Esther 3:10)
10. Mordecai (Esther 8:2)

63. They Rent Their Clothes

1. f (Gen. 37:29)
2. d (Judg. 11:31, 34–40)
3. i (II Sam. 1:11–12)
4. h (Acts 14:11–14)
5. j (Ezra 9:1–3)
6. b (II Kings 2:11–12)
7. e (Job 1:18–20)
8. c (Esther 3:12–13; 4:1)
9. g (II Chron. 23:1–13)
10. a (II Kings 22:1, 10–11)

66. Royal Apparel

1. Herod (Acts 12:20–21)
2. Saul (I Sam. 24:4)
3. Mordecai (Esther 8:2, 15)
4. Wrought gold (Ps. 45:13)
5. Gideon (Judg. 8:24–26)
6. Josiah (II Kings 22:1, 8–11)
7. Jonathan (I Sam. 18:1–4)
8. Lilies (Matt. 6:28–29)
9. David (I Chron. 15:25–28)
10. Belshazzar (Dan. 5:7, 17–29)

67. Scripture Currency

1. Mite (Mark 12:42)
2. Maneh (Ezek. 45:12)
3. Pound (Luke 19:13)
4. Brass (Matt. 10:9)
5. Talent (Matt. 18:24)
6. Penny (Matt. 22:19)
7. Dram (I Chron. 29:7)
8. Farthing (Matt. 5:26)
9. Gerah (Exod. 30:13)
10. Shekel (Gen. 23:16)

68. Shining Silver

1. j (Judg. 17:1–2)
2. g (Num. 10:1–2)
3. h (Gen. 44:2)
4. c (Acts 19:24)
5. i (Ps. 68:13)
6. a (Esther 1:2, 6)
7. e (II Sam. 8:10)
8. b (Gen. 24:52–53)
9. d (Prov. 25:11)
10. f (Isa. 40:19)

69. Ships' Parts

1. Sail (Isa. 33:23)
2. Forepart (Acts 27:41)
3. Anchor (Acts 27:29)
4. Side (Jonah 1:5)
5. Boat (Acts 27:30)
6. Helm (James 3:4)
7. Oar (Ezek. 27:6)
8. Mast (Isa. 33:23)

70. Shoes

1. g (Gen. 14:23)
2. d (Acts 12:7–8)
3. h (Josh. 5:13–15)
4. j (II Sam. 15:30)
5. i (Mark 1:6–7)
6. c (Deut. 33:1, 24–25)
7. a (Ruth 4:7–8)
8. b (Exod. 3:4–5)
9. f (Ezek. 16:10)
10. e (Amos 2:6)

71. Shut the Door

1. God (Gen. 7:16)
2. Five (Matt. 25:1–12)
3. Disciples (John 20:19)
4. Jesus (Matt. 6:6)
5. Lend a friend three loaves of bread (Luke 11:5–7)
6. Elisha (II Kings 4:1–4)
7. Paul (Acts 21:30)
8. Malachi (Mal. 1:10)
9. Lot (Gen. 19:4, 6)
10. Nehemiah (Neh. 6:10–11)

72. The Sound of Music

1. Timbrels (Judg. 11:34)
2. Cymbals (I Chron. 16:5)
3. Cornet (Ps. 98:6)
4. Harp (I Sam. 16:23)
5. Organ (Gen. 4:21)
6. Sackbut (Dan. 3:7)
7. Viol (Amos 6:5)
8. Tabrets (I Sam. 18:6)
9. Psaltery (I Sam. 10:5)
10. Trumpet (II Sam. 20:1)

73. The Sound of Trumpets

1. Moses (Num. 10:1–2)
2. Solomon (I Kings 1:39)
3. Midianites' vast army fought each other and ran away (Judg. 7:19–22)
4. 120 (II Chron. 5:12)
5. Athaliah (II Kings 11:14)
6. Seven (Josh. 6:4)
7. Sheba (II Sam. 20:1–2)
8. Paul (I Cor. 15:52)
9. Ehud (Judg. 3:25–29)
10. Joab (II Sam. 2:28)

74. Sticks and Stones

1. Isaac (Gen. 22:6)
2. David (I Sam. 17:39–40)
3. Aaron (Num. 17:8)
4. Joshua (Josh. 4:9)
5. Jacob (Gen. 30:37–38)
6. Solomon (I Kings 7:1, 9–12)
7. Moses (Exod. 4:2–3)
8. Jeremiah (Jer. 43:8–9)
9. Gideon (Judg. 6:21)
10. Samuel (I Sam. 7:12)

75. Sweet Incense

1. Nadab & Abihu (Lev. 10:1–2)
2. Ezekiel (Ezek. 8:11)
3. Zacharias (Luke 1:5–13)
4. Every morning & evening (Exod. 30:7–8)
5. Uzziah (II Chron. 26:16–21)
6. In a spoon (Num. 7:2, 14, 20, 26)
7. Aaron (Num. 16:47–48)
8. Solomon (I Kings 11:7–9)
9. John (Rev. 8:3)
10. Moses (Exod. 30:34–36)

76. Swords

1. c (II Sam. 23:9–10)
2. e (I Sam. 18:4)
3. g (John 18:10)
4. f (Exod. 17:13)
5. i (I Sam. 21:8–9)
6. h (II Sam. 20:8–10)
7. b (I Chron. 21:16)
8. j (I Sam. 17:50–51)
9. d (I Sam. 31:3–4)
10. a (Gen. 27:38–40)

77. Tabernacle Furnishings

1. Bason (Exod. 27:3)
2. Veil (Exod. 26:31)
3. Laver (Exod. 40:30)
4. Bowls (Exod. 25:29)
5. Altar (Exod. 27:1)
6. Tent (Exod. 26:11)
7. Dish (Exod. 25:29)
8. Ark (Exod. 25:10)
9. Hanging (Exod. 26:36)
10. Table (Exod. 25:23)

78. Tables

1. Adoni-bezek (Judg. 1:7)
2. Moses (Exod. 25:1, 23)
3. Shunammite woman (II Kings 4:8–10)
4. Israelites (Ps. 78:19)
5. Jesus (John 2:13–15)
6. Solomon (I Kings 7:48)
7. Lazarus (John 12:1–2)
8. Mephibosheth (II Sam. 9:6–7)
9. Jonathan (I Sam. 20:33–34)
10. Nehemiah (Neh. 5:17)

79. Talents

1. Amaziah (II Chron. 25:6)
2. Omri (I Kings 16:23–24)
3. Gehazi (II Kings 5:20–27)
4. David (II Sam. 12:29–30)
5. One (Matt. 25:24–25)
6. Hezekiah (II Kings 18:14)
7. Solomon (I Kings 10:10)
8. Zechariah (Zech. 5:7)
9. Haman (Esther 3:8–9)
10. John (Rev. 16:21)

80. The Tender Grape

1. Samson (Judg. 14:5)
2. Moses (Deut. 32:32)
3. Noah (Gen. 9:20)
4. A man may eat grapes from his neighbor's vine but may not put any in a vessel (Deut. 23:24)
5. John (Rev. 14:18–19)
6. Eshcol (Num. 13:16, 23)
7. Judah (Gen. 49:10–11)
8. Joseph (Gen. 40:9–13)
9. Naboth (I Kings 21:1–3)
10. Ezekiel (Ezek. 18:2), Jeremiah (Jer. 31:29–30)

81. Tents

1. d (Josh. 7:20–21)
2. e (Gen. 4:20)
3. g (Gen. 18:1)
4. a (Gen. 31:33–34)
5. h (Judg. 4:17–21)
6. j (Acts 18:2–3)
7. b (Judg. 7:13)
8. i (Gen. 26:17)
9. c (I Sam. 17:54)
10. f (Exod. 18:7)

82. Thorns and Briers

1. Jesus (Matt. 27:29)
2. Gideon (Judg. 8:4–7, 16)
3. Israelites (Num. 33:51–55)
4. Parable of the sower (Matt. 13:3–7)
5. Solomon (Prov. 15:19)
6. Jeremiah (Jer. 12:13)
7. Adam (Gen. 3:17–18)
8. Ezekiel (Ezek. 2:6)
9. Jotham (Judg. 9:7–15)
10. Isaiah (Isa. 34:13)

83. Thrones

1. Solomon (I Kings 10:18)
2. John (Rev. 4:3)
3. Twelve (Matt. 19:28)
4. Nebuchadnezzar (Jer. 43:9–10)
5. The throne of his father David (Luke 1:32)
6. Jeremiah (Jer. 3:17)
7. Bathsheba (I Kings 2:18–19)
8. Daniel (Dan. 7:9)
9. Herod (Acts 12:21–23)
10. King of Israel—Ahab, Jehoshaphat (I Kings 22:10)

84. "Thy Rod and Thy Staff"

1. David (I Sam. 17:40)
2. Zechariah (Zech. 11:7)
3. Twelve (Num. 17:6–7)
4. Jacob (Gen. 32:9, 10)
5. Jonathan (I Sam. 14:27)
6. Gehazi (II Kings 4:29)
7. Moses (Exod. 4:2–3)
8. Gideon (Judg. 6:19, 21)
9. Aaron (Num. 17:8)
10. David (Ps. 23:4)

85. Treasure Hunt

1. Golden calf (Exod. 32:2–4)
2. Silver and gold (Gen. 13:2)
3. Gold earring (Job 42:11)
4. Gold chain (Dan. 5:29)
5. Spices, gold, and precious stones (I Kings 10:1–2)
6. Two bracelets (Gen. 24:22)
7. Crown (Esther 2:17)
8. Twelve precious stones (Exod. 28:17–21)
9. Pearl (Matt. 13:45–46)
10. Gold, frankincense, and myrrh (Matt. 2:7–11)

86. Trees

1. d (II Sam. 5:23–24)
2. e (Luke 19:2–4)
3. g (Judg. 4:4–5)
4. a (II Sam. 18:10)
5. h (I Sam. 14:2)
6. j (I Kings 5:10)
7. b (John 1:48)
8. i (I Chron. 27:28)
9. c (I Kings 19:4)
10. f (II Chron. 9:11)

87. Veils

1. When giving God's instructions to Israelites (Exod. 34:32–33)
2. The holy place and most holy place (Exod. 26:31–33)
3. Any with a physical defect (Lev. 21:16–23)
4. Cover the ark with it (Num. 4:5)
5. Linen (II Chron. 3:14)
6. Rebekah (Gen. 24:64–65)
7. Boaz (Ruth 3:15)
8. Isaiah (Isa. 3:16, 18, 23)
9. When Jesus was crucified (Matt. 27:50–51)
10. Paul (II Cor. 3:13–16)

88. Windows

1. Jezebel (II Kings 9:30–33)
2. Sisera's mother (Judg. 5:28)
3. Rahab (Josh. 2:15)
4. Noah (Gen. 8:6–7)
5. Solomon (Prov. 7:6–7)
6. Joash (II Kings 13:14–17)
7. Daniel (Dan. 6:10)
8. Paul (II Cor. 11:33)
9. Eutychus (Acts 20:7)
10. Michal (II Sam. 6:16)

89. Wood

1. j (II Sam. 6:5)
2. g (Num. 17:8)
3. h (Gen. 30:37–38)
4. c (I Kings 7:1–3)
5. i (Gen. 6:14)
6. a (Exod. 37:1, 10)
7. e (Neh. 8:4)
8. b (Gen. 22:2–3)
9. d (Jer. 27:2; 28:10)
10. f (I Chron. 21:23)

90. What Became of These?

1. His brothers stained it with goat's blood and gave it to his father (Gen. 37:31–32)
2. Came to rest upon the mountains of Ararat (Gen. 8:4)
3. The soldiers cast lots for it at His crucifixion (John 19:23–24)
4. Broken in pieces by King Hezekiah (II Kings 18:1, 4)
5. Elisha inherited it (II Kings 2:13–14)
6. Ceased when they reached Canaan (Exod. 16:35)
7. Burned to ground by Nebuchadnezzar's soldiers (II Kings 25:1, 8–9)
8. Ahimelech gave it to David (I Sam. 21:8–9)
9. Chief priests and elders used the money to buy a potters field (Matt. 27:3–7)
10. Moses burned the calf in fire, ground it to powder, spread it upon water, and made the Israelites drink it (Exod. 32:20)